Your Towns and Cities in the Great War

Harrogate and Ripon
in the Great War

Your Towns and Cities in the Great War

Harrogate and Ripon in the Great War

Stephen Wade

Pen & Sword
MILITARY

First published in Great Britain in 2016 by
PEN & SWORD MILITARY
an imprint of
Pen and Sword Books Ltd
47 Church Street
Barnsley
South Yorkshire S70 2AS

ISBN 978 1 47385 555 7

A CIP record for this book is available from the British Library

Printed and bound in England
by CPI Group (UK) Ltd, Croydon, CR0 4YY

Typeset in Times New Roman by Chic Graphics

Pen & Sword Books Ltd incorporates the imprints of
Pen & Sword Archaeology, Atlas, Aviation, Battleground, Discovery,
Family History, History, Maritime, Military, Naval, Politics, Railways,
Select, Social History, Transport, True Crime, Claymore Press,
Frontline Books, Leo Cooper, Praetorian Press, Remember When,
Seaforth Publishing and Wharncliffe.

For a complete list of Pen and Sword titles please contact
Pen and Sword Books Limited
47 Church Street, Barnsley, South Yorkshire, S70 2AS, England
E-mail: enquiries@pen-and-sword.co.uk
Website: www.pen-and-sword.co.uk

Contents

Acknowledgements

Many people have helped in the research for this book. David Knight, archivist at Stonyhurst College, helped with the De Trafford material; Greta Hills was very much my Ripon researcher; at Harrogate, Nicola Baxter and Sheila Asante at the Pump Room Museum helped with the use of materials from their exhibition on Harrogate at War. Also, Linne Matthews and Roni Wilkinson were a great support. Anyone writing on Harrogate has a debt of gratitude to Malcolm Neesam, who is very much the doyen of historians on that town. Other experts provided commentary and footnotes, notably Bryan Longbone who is always my railway correspondent in any local history project.

For help in acquiring some of the Ripon material, thanks go once more to Greta Hills and also the headmaster of Ripon Grammar School.

The Barnbow references owe a lot to Ann Batchelor but there appears to be nothing in print that I can source, so I have to thank her in respect of reports from the many talks she has given on the disaster at Crossgates.

For the value of having sources from the *Harrogate Herald* available on the net, thanks go to Tony Cheal whose labours in that area have been an immeasurable help, along with the Harrogate Central Library staff and their compilation of very full listings of local men and their war destinations held in the reference library.

For help with some of the more ephemeral publications, thanks go to staff at the Brynmor Jones Library, University of Hull.

Material relating to the Khaki University of Canada was accessed with the help of staff at the War Museum of Canada. The picture of Lieutenant Colonel Gerald Birks and his fellow officers of the YMCA is by courtesy of Springfield College, Babson Library, Archives and Special Collections.

Some of the more detailed biographical profiles were only possible with help from family historians and I must thank Martin Birtle particularly in this respect.

Finally, I thank Dr Roger Kendall for his detective work on the Owen *Schoolmistress* poem and the Ripon School. Walking the roads by that junction today gives one a very clear impression of Owen's time there.

Introduction

When a writer first begins to look at the potential sources for yet another book devoted to the Great War, there is a nagging sense that maybe the reading public has had enough, particularly during this centenary period. However, that is simply a transient thought; those four years of horrendous conflict go on and on spinning new stories. The more we look back the deeper the scrutiny and the surprising accounts of sheer grit and endurance still move us. As I write this, it is almost exactly 100 years since the Battle of Neuve Chapelle, at which that little settlement was taken at a cost of 12,000 British casualties. Consequently, when I think of that statistic I know that there can never be enough in print, on film or on the air regarding that mammoth conflict in which so many thousands paid the ultimate price. Like the annual poppy sales, wreath-laying and parades, the print relating to that war must go on, expanding and filling in the details. That literature is a vital part of our ongoing tribute to the fallen.

Strangely, sometimes a book is conceived from a shred of anecdote and this is one of them. In fact there were two stories, each highlighting different aspects of war.

The first concerns a family story. I was talking with other writers about the novelist Elizabeth Elgin who lived near Ripon and someone brought to mind the story of her gamekeeper father. He was in the firing squad detailed to shoot a young lad who had run from battle in 1915. She recalled how her father knew he was the only one in the squad who knew how to shoot to kill. Not only does the anecdote show how one man's theatre of heroic war is another man's scene of despicable murder, it also provides the start of my research into the material for this book. The main reason for this is that Ripon will always be associated with the emergence of the Pals battalions – Kitchener's

'New Army' – because of the camp at that town which was the focus of training for the Northern Command.

The second story came from my research for a book on the conscientious objectors of the Great War. I came across the sad story of Ernest England and his story made me see how pivotal Ripon was in that complex web of bases, camps and training grounds that covered Britain at the time. He had been interned after refusing to join up and was at Ripon when he received the news that his mother in Leeds was dying. John Graham, writing in 1922, tells the tale:

> A telephone message from the family to the Brigadier-General in charge resulted in leave being granted to return home for twenty four hours under escort. No trains were running at that late hour, and it was necessary to find a taxi-cab to Leeds at double fare... He arrived a few hours before the death of his mother...

England himself was to die in Dartmoor not long after.

These two stories showed me just how much the Harrogate and Ripon area had played a part in the war: the first was a fragment of family oral history and the second was one of those submerged narratives that are there, parallel to the big picture but seldom told.

However, there is a deeper layer of interest in a book that features so much about the 'Pals'; the sheer transmutation of innocence into extreme experience through a test of manhood and courage that is hard to find anywhere else in history. As Herbert Read, a native of a part of North Yorkshire just a short way up the A1 from Ripon, working on his war diary: 'At the outbreak of war a man should be thankful if he can retain any kind of identity – if he can act as an individual rather than be swept down the stream of national hysteria.'

Rupert Brooke put it more succinctly, when asked by J.C. Squire why he was rushing to war. He answered: 'Well, if Armageddon is on... I suppose one should be there!'

There is also the geographical point to make. In the ancient wapentake of Claro, which covers present-day Harrogate and Knaresborough, the northern areas, around Burton Leonard and Roecliffe, are very nearly in Ripon. Therefore I had a decision to make regarding which places to foreground. In the end I decided to include

Knaresborough with Harrogate but merely for historical purposes. To use the word Claro would have made sense, as Ripon Liberty sits closely alongside the divisions of the lower and upper ancient wapentake. In other words, in terms of a book about the Great War and these places, no conveniently brief overall term could easily be used.

Growing up in Leeds in the 1950s, I was told that Harrogate folk were 'posh'. One joke around my part of the Leeds suburbs was that Harrogate housewives soap-stoned their doorsteps in fancy patterns. However, that was a working-class view and it came from the experience of visiting Harrogate, just 17 miles up the road from Moortown; a trip that usually entailed a visit to Betty's Tea Room and the splendidly impressive cluster of old Georgian buildings with grand, imposing and proud facades. Later, I came to think of Harrogate's special blend of beauty and hard stone as being the essence of my Yorkshire.

In my teens I was a regular visitor to the Harrogate Theatre, and the richness of the town's particular identity won me over. I watched a succession of Bernard Shaw plays, went to musical concerts, and stood in awe at the massive gritty strength and symmetry in the architecture. In my writing life, it would not be any stretch of the truth to say that Harrogate became my spiritual home.

Another reason for this was that Ripon, a few miles further north, also offered me something special: Wilfred Owen, the quintessential poet of war, had been billeted there in the war against the Kaiser. He was one of my inspirational figures, just as he had been to many young men in the 1920s that had missed what Christopher Isherwood described as 'The Test': taking part in that Armageddon in France as a trial of their true manhood.

Consequently, when I discovered that Pen & Sword had created a series on towns in the Great War, my immediate thought was to place the two towns together and tell their stories of the years 1914–19. That war had the effect of stretching and distorting local geography as men in various battalions were intertwined, passing through the great camps at Ripon or through the hospitals in Harrogate. The memoirs of men in the Pals battalions in particular present the historian with a complex chronology of camaraderie as men from Barnsley and Grimsby, or from Hull and Leeds, rubbed shoulders in camp. In fact, on the surface of history, the two towns are potentially defined in their Great War roles by the words 'hospitals' and 'camps'. Of course that is a simplification, but with so many books on the shelves dealing with the Pals and the Chums, the general perception is understandable.

A considerable portion of this book will build on the solid groundwork done on the volunteer army of 1914 by a number of writers, many of their stories brought together in Roni Wilkinson's study *Pals on the Somme 1916*. I am aware that, in recounting the experience of the soldiers at the Ripon camps, I am reinforcing the impressions gathered in a series of books dealing with the subject but Ripon itself, and the way it coped, is open to study. The army camps at that time had a massive local impact. The camp outside Grantham, for instance, where a huge number of troops created a social problem, played an incidental part in the creation of our women's police force as female officers were instrumental in dealing with the difficulties there. Ripon similarly saw the potential negative effects of having so many troops nearby. Consequently, military and social histories interact.

In fact, as a preliminary survey shows, there are multiple stories around the two Yorkshire towns in that huge struggle of the great powers. As with all human history, the events are bundles of biographies with strange and fascinating intermixtures, such as the fact that J.R.R. Tolkien was briefly staying in Harrogate during his army years, or that a Russian Grand Duchess decided her vocation was to care for the Tommies at that huge moment in British history.

The Great War stories of the two towns, as expected, provide profound personal tragedies as well as formidable achievements in conflict, such as the sad death of Captain Thomas de Trafford of Rudding Park and the VC winner Charles Hull who distinguished himself on the North-West Frontier of India in 1915, taking not only the VC but also the French Croix de Guerre. He was one of three men from the area who won VCs and naturally their stories will feature in these pages.

However, it was total war. We see the chain of events – from the declaration of war with Germany in August 1914 to the last demobilizations in 1919 – as a complex affair, triggered by the assassination of an emperor by a Serbian nationalist; we see it as grainy old film of intense suffering in mud-washed trenches; we see it in documentaries about the sinking of the *Lusitania* and the outrages committed against shopkeepers with German surnames. Most of all we see that unique and horrifying confrontation as a massive, all-embracing epic of sacrifice and nobility. Looking deeper, we might easily discern the underbelly of that era: the cruelty handed out to those who would not fight for conscientious reasons and the deprivations at home when families could starve and thousands died in the raging pandemic of influenza in 1918 and 1919.

Now, however, we need to look closer, taking the lens near to these two towns and their condition on the eve of the supposed 'war to end wars'.

What was Harrogate like at the turn of the century, in those years before the war that would rattle the whole of the British Empire and involve millions of ordinary people from Russia to Paris and from Australasia to Africa in turmoil and suffering? A publication of 1886, *Thorpe's Illustrated Guide to Harrogate*, foregrounds the same things that such guides do now: the mineral springs, the 'bracing nature of the climate' and the 'invigorating freshness and salubrity of its air.' However, the guide also notes that the town 'had trebled its resident population and increased its visitors fourfold in the last quarter of a century.'

To most people, Harrogate meant a spa and Ripon meant the cathedral. Beyond that, many aspects of both towns were related systematically to their two defining features. Yet Harrogate by the end of the nineteenth century was one of the noted places for a healthy and wealthy middle-class lifestyle. The publications of commerce and advertising at that time reflect a place in which Walter Davey, 'high class portraiture', offered twelve *cartes de visite* at 9 shillings; Ace Terry had the skills to re-cover your umbrella; and Mr W. Hardy of Volta House could provide any kind of electro-plating one might desire.

Clearly, a town renowned for its healthy springs and water treatments had to have hotels and high-class lodging houses along with hospitals and convalescent homes. *Robinson's Harrogate Directory* of 1910 lists eight such institutions, ranging from the Harrogate Infirmary to the Primitive Methodist orphanages. It was even the seat of the Northern Police Orphanage which provided 'a Home, with maintenance, clothing, education, training etc' and the Northern Police Convalescent Home which catered for 'police officers of all ranks needing rest and change of air after sickness or injury.' There were some truly magnificent hotels for the wealthier clients who had come for the waters and good air: a typically impressive example was the Prospect Hotel (which became the Imperial in 1988) that had been constructed way back in 1814. In 1870 it was greatly enlarged with the addition of a substantial tower, and the Carter family, who had owned it from its beginning, remained in control until 1936.

Not long after the war, in the 1920s, in the Ward Lock *Guide to Harrogate* the business directory section provides a useful profile of the town's prominence as a place for convalescence. A typical example from among many is the Wellington Hotel: 'Two minutes to Pump Room and Baths and five minutes to Royal Hall. Every modern convenience. Lift to all floors.' The same publication lists nineteen hotels and three specialist hydropathic establishments. The author claims that ailments mitigated by the Harrogate waters included skin diseases, liver disorders, gout, rheumatism, nervous exhaustion, scrofula, lumbago, anaemia, chronic bronchitis and malaria.

A few years after the war, the *Medical Annual* carried a feature making it clear that Harrogate was far more than just a pleasant place to rest. The general manager of the Harrogate spas made sure that his advert was impressive: 'Empirical methods do not obtain at Harrogate. A lengthy and very exhaustive SCIENTIFIC INVESTIGATION into the Harrogate waters... has just been completed and all their recommendations put into force...'

Just fifteen years after the war, a book giving a 'tour' of Yorkshire described Harrogate's status well: 'Harrogate today is one of Yorkshire's achievements. Its great hotels and hydros, its shops and schools, medicinal baths and Valley Gardens are a tangible proof that it has arrived.' The same work's verdict on neighbouring Ripon was equally complimentary and stressed the picturesque: 'There is a Dales feeling in the villages clustering around it; West Tanfield with its houses along the banks of the Ure, and Marmion tower, the gatehouse of the Marmions and the Fitzhughs, standing by the church...'

Of course, there was far more to Ripon than that. Its marquis was not only a major employer but also someone who typified the manners and mores of the aristocracy of his time and whose hobbies ironically anticipated mass-scale shooting in war; in 1894 he and his friends went out with shotguns on several occasions and clocked up 19,000 dead hares in that year. This was a piece of the old pre-war world that was to change with the conflict.

There was also something very distinctively literary about Ripon at the time of the Great War. Not only were Wilfred Owen and J.B. Priestley there as soldiers but it was also the birthplace of Naomi Jacob, and the poet and critic Herbert Read was also fairly local, not so far north. Naomi's father was headmaster at Ripon Grammar School and she was to live in the city until the age of 14.

The town was well aware of the charms of its neighbour. As David Raw has pointed out, Ripon was ambitious and reacting to its close neighbour at the time war broke out: attempts had been made to stimulate the local economy by setting up a spa to rival Harrogate immediately before the war. In 1900 the radical Marquess of Ripon of Studley Royal had sold land for a spa pump room and pleasure gardens.

However, in August 1914, along with the rest of Britain, these two beautiful towns, rich in cultural history, were to be rocked by the threat of war. The following chapters give an account of their place in that conflict with Germany and her allies, and after investigating that history I am certain that this contribution to the great, overarching narrative of the Great War will assert their importance in the broader context.

Note: Two Invaluable Sources
Anyone undertaking research into these two places cannot possibly avoid two men in particular: one who orchestrated communication between home and battlefield throughout the war years and one who is very much an active historian today. Something must be said at the outset about their importance.

W.H. Breare: Harrogate
Anyone writing about or researching Harrogate in the Great War will find it utterly impossible to avoid meeting the writings of William Hammond Breare, editor of the *Harrogate Herald* for many decades. There is surely no other local newspaper issued during the years 1914−18 that had such a pivotal and influential figure co-ordinating communications between home and the theatre of war.

Breare was born in the United States and came to England as a music student. Indeed, he was prominent in the Harrogate music scene for many years and is the author of *Vocal Faults and Their Remedies* (1907). However, for the historian wanting to understand the Great War, he was the writer of the weekly column 'To Our Boys in Service' in which he dealt with requests, shortages and general topics of interest. His name will run throughout my book as a constant source of material.

Breare was a successor of Robert Ackrill, who died in 1894 and was the founder of the *Herald* printing works, and also a man who worked for the charter of incorporation for Harrogate. Breare was surely a 'founding father' of Harrogate social and historical writing; a man for whom no subject was too trivial or marginal when it came to helping the men in khaki who had left their jobs to fight the Kaiser.

Peter Liddle: Ripon

In a feature in the *Harrogate Advertiser* in August 2014, tribute was paid to Dr Peter Liddle who was then leading a study conference at Weetwood Hall on the Great War. He spoke to the press about his interest in the history of this great conflict and how he worked hard to preserve the memories of people who had participated. He said: 'I was a young schoolmaster and I soon realized that I had been given a great gift of awareness that history was all around me. However, I was appalled at the destruction and loss of evidence of our past that was happening right in front of me.' He started to record survivors and the result, eventually, was the Liddle Collection now kept at the Brotherton Library at the University of Leeds. This massive resource contains thousands of diaries and letters from the war years.

Peter Liddle is a resident of Ripon and the press report rightly used the word 'crusade' with regard to what he has been doing as a historian, now for several decades. He explained the impetus behind his dedication to capturing textless history by saying: 'If we don't have respect for our past, how can we sensibly manage our present if there's an absence of understanding?'

His indefatigable labours have led to that priceless resource for future writers and historians to access, and of course it all offers something very different from second-hand collections of material. The soldiers are speaking directly, as it were, with first-person reports of their experiences.

CHAPTER 1

1914
The Call for
Kitchener's Army

On 4 August 1914, soldiers of the Kaiser's army moved into Belgium. The dominant master plan of the German military strategists was labelled the Schlieffen Plan, having the aim of advancing forces into Belgium and Northern France. A further flank of the army was destined to move on Paris. One of the most powerful elements in this, as far as Britain was concerned, was that the might of Germany was about to crush 'little neutral Belgium' and the might of the British Empire was honour-bound to act, rather than stand by and watch a massacre.

On the date that war with Germany was announced, there was a quick response in terms of mobilizing what forces were available in the professional full-time army in Britain. For decades there had been a growing number of Reservists – the volunteer battalions – and their moment had arrived. A glance at popular magazines such as *The Graphic* throughout the 1880s to the 1910s immediately gives the reader an insight into this culture of amateur soldiers. Rifle practice, drilling and indeed 'war games' – a concept invented by the Germans back in the 1870s – are described in that press. Boys and young men, in activities ranging from cadet forces to Territorials, were military-minded. More than that, journals such as *The Strand* and the Harmsworth publications through those years were crammed with features on warships, heroic officers, guns and new projected technological topics of war.

The response may be assessed and understood in a number of ways but one angle on this, explained by John Sadler and Rosie Serdiville, is helpful here: 'For the British, the idea of conscription was anathema: free men enlisted because it was right, not because the state compelled. Never before in history, and probably never again, was the road to war so heavily subscribed.'

We know the manpower in question here. In one history of the West Riding troops we have some statistics on the Territorials:

> When the mass-problem was approached by Lord Harewood, as Lieutenant of the Riding, there were 18,300 of all ranks. On March 31st, 1908 the actual strength of those old forces was 414 officers and 9,683 other ranks; so that, roughly, 8,000 in all had to be found additionally in the West Riding.

The underlying assumption was a concept to be severely ironical when the 1916 Military Service Act came along and introduced conscription: Colonel Land of the Territorials summed up the assumption with the words 'The word "conscription" appears to be repulsive to the vast majority of Englishmen.' How acutely this was to be affirmed in 1916 compared with the mass enlistment of 1914 is shown by the turmoil involved in dealing with the conscientious objectors of the latter year.

Yet this would not provide the manpower: this reserve base would not be enough, Lord Kitchener and his War Cabinet knew, to take on the might of Germany in an infantry war. Before recruitment began and the banners with 'Your Country Needs You' proliferated, there was one initial military manoeuvre: the British Expeditionary Force swung into action. British troops set foot in France by 7 August and on the 23rd of that month at the Battle of Mons, at which the Germans had more men in the field but could not fully triumph, the British rapid fire held sway and the general feeling after that first encounter was that Britain would acquit herself well. There was talk of the war being over by Christmas. However, the call to arms accelerated.

Not everyone in the higher echelons of power saw the 'citizen recruits' as providing the answer to all military problems. Brigadier Henry Wilson (later killed by the Irish nationalists) wrote:

THERE'S A VACANT PLACE FOR **YOU** MY LAD!

YOUR KING AND COUNTRY NEED YOU

Lord Kitchener has obtained 900,000 recruits, and only 100,000 are needed to make up the first million. So take *your* place in the ranks, young man, at once, and enlist at the nearest recruiting office, for the sake of your King and Country.

A comic cartoon showing a recruiting scene. (Evening Telegraph)

Can't the b—— fools at home realize that we are fighting against a perfectly glorious army led by real generals and soldiers, and that nothing but the best is of any use whatever. Kitchener's shadow armies, for shadow campaigns at unknown dates are becoming a positive danger, as they rob us of good officers and men.

Yet who would listen to such opinions in the climate of August 1914, when 'little Belgium' needed us?

There were also people around who maintained critical attitudes, recalling the immense loss of life in the wars with the Boers in South Africa when young men had been cut down in their thousands. Marie Corelli, the novelist, published a tract with that spirit, concluding: 'Make him a hero of the home and the heart, not of the music hall. And when the dance of the society clowns is done; when they have finally retired from the wearied public view...tell us that our brave dead...' So the dissenting voices were there but the euphoria won the day.

Still, some influential writers explained, for the 'common man', what the situation with Germany was. Robert Blatchford, a widely-read *Daily Mail* writer, put it to his readers in the mode of a teacher with an elementary class:

> Germany is preparing to attack us because we stand in the way of her ambitions. The ambition of the Pan-Germans, who are the war party, who are the masters of Germany, is no new thing in world history; it is a very old thing, as old as it is evil. For the Pan-Germanic ambition to dominate and exploit the world. It is the old, old Lust for power and glory, the old, old greed for trade and wealth.

People were in no doubt that the North Sea and the coasts were going to be crucially important in this war. As Blatchford put it: 'Germany sorely needs more ports, a greater seaboard.' A general worry was would the great British navy be enough? Writers, as war was in the air, had pointed out that nations bordering Germany were panicking; we had the Channel and that was a bulwark but it was not total protection. The German fleet had been developing for decades.

Shortly before Christmas, the potential for naval attack turned into an actual bombardment. On Wednesday, 16 December, Colina Campbell, a Harrogate girl serving as a Voluntary Aid Detachment nurse, was near Whitby and she wrote home:

> Two German cruisers fired at the coastguard station, shot that to bits and killed one coastguard; we saw the stretcher being carried. Some of the coastguards said the cruisers came in so close they could see the men working on the decks. We hear that the cruisers visited Scarborough and other places and damaged them...

She also gave a very close-up account of the material effects of the bombings: 'Telegraph wires hanging like threads all snapped, huge gaping holes in the side of houses, roofs off, glass smashed everywhere and old women shaking with fright and sobbing. We picked up lots of bits of shell. I have one in my pocket as I write...'

Colina had indeed witnessed a large-scale attack, as a warning of the struggle to come across the North Sea and beyond. The *Daily Mail* reported that the Germans had bombarded three English towns and announced that there had been forty-four killed and sixty-six injured. Colina's account was amplified: 'At Whitby two battle cruisers fired some shots, doing damage to buildings and the following casualties are reported: two killed and two wounded.'

Before the new recruits lined up, the Territorials acted; on 15 August the 5th West Yorkshires left York. The local paper reported that the Harrogate, Knaresborough and Ripon companies were 'going under canvas in a field off Leeds Road. Their work of recruiting has been proceeding briskly at York headquarters...' The route marches and field drilling were to begin in earnest.

Inevitably, the Chums were created. By September, working men of all kinds had lined up at the recruiting offices after standing in crowds listening to speakers describing the Belgian atrocities and the bestiality of 'the Hun'. There was a public meeting in Knaresborough on 15 September and the *Harrogate Herald* described the scene, which was attended by the High Sheriff of Yorkshire, C.E. Charlesworth, along with members of the aristocracy and principal churchmen. The sheriff summed up the atmosphere in a way that must have been repeated across the land: 'The Chairman said he did not remember when he could recall an occasion in his long life when he presided over a meeting of extraordinary anxiety and importance.'

The themes were familiar to the crowd from the daily papers: the demand of a sacrifice; the support of Belgium; the necessity for honourable behaviour; the cry for help from their king; and the urgency of the need to confront the Kaiser. Applause interspersed the speeches, which were drenched in passionate rhetoric. The Reverend Father Vaughan appears to have been a star in these skills, as the *Herald* man reported:

> Our watchword was for protection and civilization and to protect the weak against the strong, and if the bulls were out, Germans would have to meet John Bull's men (applause). They were called by their King and country and for the great Principles of truth, honour and freedom. Never had men rallied so well to the flag and never had England been so unanimous or determined...

An unknown soldier, new to the uniform, in camp. (Author's own)

He ended his speech with a call 'to the young men of Knaresborough and Yorkshire to respond to Lord Kitchener's appeal for men in the name of truth, justice, freedom...'

The spirit of the time is caught perfectly in the rhymes of Jessie Pope, as in these stanzas from *The Blackest Lie* (1915):

> Hurry with the whitewash,
> Pour it out in streams!
> Bleach the ravaged country,
> Louvain, Antwerp, Rheims!

> Belgium concocted war
> Thus deserves her fate!
> That's the blackest Teuton lie
> Published up to date.

Recruiting meetings were to go on through the autumn. A typical one was held on the High Street in Knaresborough in late November, with the drums and bugles of the 5th Reserve Battalion standing by. Speaking to the crowd were a British officer, Captain Kelley, and a Belgian officer, Lieutenant Heynrick.

The *Harrogate Advertiser* announced the call to arms with all the basic information required:

> An addition of 100,000 men to His Majesty's Army is immediately necessary in the present grave national emergency. Lord Kitchener is confident that this appeal will be at once responded to by all those who have the safety of the Empire at heart. TERMS OF SERVICE: General service for a period of 3 years or until the war is concluded. Age of enlistment between 19 and 30.

Who was this Kitchener, staring out at the recruits from the posters? Herbert Kitchener, surely best known as the stern face on the Great War poster proclaiming 'Your Country Needs You', was a great military leader who seemed to attract controversy as well as hagiography and myth. One early biographer, writing in 1910, expressed the complexity: 'That he wields some strange and subtle power over the crowd is indisputable. The secret of it may lie in the awe inspired by those marvellous successes he never fails to produce by the magic of his patient persistence…' Notice here the words 'awe' and 'magic' placed alongside words that are not directly heroic.

His legendary steely eyes and dignified bearing could instil fear and he was seen by some as ruthless. However, at the field of Omdurman (1898) it was Kitchener who commanded the people of the town to go out and bring in the wounded from the field. Estimates of him vary greatly, but perhaps Richard Holmes' words in the *Oxford Companion to Military History* form the best appraisal: 'Kitchener was an indefatigable organizer who understood the absolute necessity of

An advert for Chums *magazine ('Chums' being the name used for some of the Pals battalions). (Author's own)*

Kitchener, the King, and the Prince of Wales.

Herbert Kitchener. (Author's own)

consolidating resources before striking a decisive blow.' On the other hand, Erskine Childers' opinion was that 'Kitchener was inclined to think too much of propelling and too little of educating his army – to look rather to the quantity rather than the quality of the work done…'

Kitchener was a strategist and a man with a presence in a battlefield.

When events were developing in the process of a confrontation, he would appear at just the right time. He was expert in what we might call today the logistics of managing men, supplies and communications. More than anything else, it could be argued, he inspired men; he glowed with confidence, with the assurance that comes from good planning and research. From Wolseley he learned that the time given to finding the right man for the job is the secret of success. When the journalist G.W. Steevens went with the Sudan expedition in 1898, working on what would become the best-selling *With Kitchener to Khartoum* (1898), he wrote that the great general should be a national treasure, or in the words of the time, something that should be exhibited at a national exhibition:

> But it so happens that he has turned himself to the management
> of war in the Sudan, and he is the complete and only master of
> that art. Beginning life in the Royal Engineers… he early turned
> to the study of the Levant. He was one of Beaconsfield's military
> vice-consuls in Asia Minor; he was subsequently director of the
> Palestine Exploration Fund… The ripe harvest of fifteen years
> is that he knows everything that is to be learned of his subject…
> He came at the right hour. He was the right man.

This was the national celebrity who seemed to personify the tough determination of the British spirit; the will and resolve that had won the Empire and wanted to keep it. He was 'Kitchener of Khartoum' because he had won back that city in the Sudan after General Gordon had been cut down there and the forces of the Mahdi had taken a British-held location of some importance.

Kitchener knew his military psychology. He and his confrères knew that men best face the enemy and cope with all the arduous secondary duties of soldiering when they are with their mates. The notion was that the same bonding that is evident in the amateur football teams across the country would be the cement of the essential *esprit de corps* in war. If men could join and know that they were to remain with their workmates, then the psychology of the crowd, of the pack, would win the day. It was thought that this spirit of facing death together had defeated the Zulu at Rorke's Drift in 1879 and had eventually triumphed in the Anglo-Boer Wars of 1899–1902.

The enlistment could be seen, with hindsight, as a call to an exciting adventure; a natural progression from the reading of periodicals and papers about the adventures of 'Chums' in those far-off outposts of Empire where men were called to show their bravery and resolve. Novels with 'chums' in the title had been popular for decades and the ideology of clannish allegiance was firmly in the male mind.

There are not too many records in the category of oral history around from this time in Ripon but one outstanding instance of this is a memoir by Jim Gott, who was born in 1897, and he recalled the mood of the time, talking about a local man known as 't'Admiral':

> During the First World War, he would go up to any male of likely service age, and prod him with a stick, demanding, 'And why aren't you in the forces my man?' Well do I remember him doing this to a pal of mine, who, being confronted with the usual prod and demand, promptly pulled up his trousers and answered, 'Yer know Admiral, yer don't git these wi' soap coupons!' – revealing an artificial leg.

The local men who ran to join these groups, known as the Pals battalions, experienced much the same as their contemporaries across the country: the rigours of enlistment, with the medical examinations and queuing, together with the bafflement at all things military. Then followed the marches through the towns and the parades and speeches. This first phase was all about euphoria: the young men from desks, workshops and coal mines were to be soldiers carrying bayonetted rifles; they were the object of female adoration and general approbation. No white feathers were placed in matchboxes and handed to them. All this marching and posturing was done, as far as the Chums were concerned, without proper military uniform and without weapons at first.

The groundwork for this attitude to soldiering was there from boyhood, in the popular reading available for boys. Denis Healey, brought up in Riddlesden, described this well in his autobiography: 'My love for the sentimental patriotism of Buchan and Newbolt was a natural legacy of the First World War, and was fed by the boys' magazines – above all by the enormous *Chums* annuals, which carried long serials about the dastardly Huns...'

The men who came in their thousands to the Ripon camps had biographical profiles that show all the aspects of recruitment that we think of now when the events of the Great War are retold. Typical of those who joined the ranks under age (and who was probably told to walk around a field and then when he returned he would be old enough) was Thomas Wybert Birtle, who joined the Durham Light Infantry. He was only 15 when he joined. As his grandson Martin wrote: 'At some point young Thomas was recognized by an officer as being under-age and he was promptly sent back to England.' However, he returned later, then with the Highland Light Infantry, and saw plenty of action and had interesting experiences. As Martin added:

> Later in the war the Highland Light Infantry were in the trenches at St Quentain, in 1918. Thomas Birtle was a sergeant at this stage, in charge of a full platoon, at the tender age of 18. The artillery had been laying down a rolling barrage, which in theory should have cut through the barbed wire in front of the German trenches... but now all was quiet on that sector of the Western Front.

There would have been hundreds of men spending time at Ripon, learning their soldiering, who were to have that adventurous trajectory of experience in front of them. As for Thomas, he survived the war and was in the Home Guard during the next big war.

The back-up was there. Those who could afford it could call in at Greensmith's shop in Harrogate and buy Burberry war kit, everything from greatcoats to weatherproofs. The advertisements proclaimed 'The Burberry sheds rain and never becomes sodden and heavy. Its materials are porous to air, so that it maintains healthful warmth.'

Fundamental to all the workings of support was fund-raising. At one extreme there were the general schemes for raising money led by newspapers and firms; at the other there were individuals such as Mr S.M. Bryde of Kirkman Bank who offered a bonus of £3 to every man in Knaresborough who enlisted and was accepted into Kitchener's army.

There was also the YMCA, which had been founded by George Williams in 1844. The organization had created a World Alliance by 1905, and its first hostels were built in Britain in 1912 at Cardiff and London. In 1914, the YMCA quickly initiated the establishment of a

An advert for military dress in Harrogate. (The Times)

network of huts which would be at camps, both at home and in the theatre of war; there was also a programme of education, and in the familiarly-marked 'red triangle' hut the Tommy could find company, tea, food and even a book-room. Harrogate had its own Great War heroine from the ranks of the YMCA in Betty Stevenson, and her story will be told when the year 1918 is recounted.

Help was needed for the refugees from Belgium and there was a steady flow of these poor people coming for shelter, care and food. They were dispersed across the land and around Harrogate and Ripon some 400 of them were catered for. They needed rent-free accommodation and the good people of the area stepped forward. In Ripon, homes were found in Park Street and in Bondgate, and of course, as one might expect, hotels also played a part with the Spa Hotel taking some in.

One outstanding figure in this essential charity work was Father Ernest Levick who was priest at St Wilfred's church; he was particularly useful as he spoke Flemish and he also used to give the children lessons at the church school. One notable cultural aspect of the Belgians' stay in Ripon was their production of toys as they made such items as little boxes, and perhaps most significant of all they made Noah's arks, one of which was sent to Queen Mary.

The question of normal life and general disruption has to arise when we recall the magnitude of the war. Malcolm Neesam, in his account of the Majestic Hotel, describes the nature of the new conditions and how they affected the tenor of life: 'Uniforms everywhere, guests on leave from the services, visitors enjoying a few hours' relaxation before resuming duties, stories, gossip, tales of missing men, accounts of valour, pain, hope and despair, telegrams received, telegrams expected.'

Harrogate was always a place of hotels of course, and Malcolm Neesam explains a footnote to social history in this context that says a great deal about the effects of war:

> The war years saw the end of the practice which went back a century. It had been the habit of all Harrogate hotels and guest houses to publish the names and home towns of visitors. These lists of visitors formed the principal content of the earliest newspapers, their purpose being to enable guests at one establishment to learn of the existence of any family and friends who might be staying at another address... However, in 1916 the lists disappeared, possibly because of paper shortages...

Resources and aid were everywhere encouraged and developed. One paper feature summed up the mood, again referring to Knaresborough:

The Majestic Hotel: a home for servicemen. (Author's own)

'Whether in sending recruits, caring for the wounded heroes, housing the refugees, or helping the national funds, Knaresborough has rendered willing service, and is worthy of all honour.'

The camps at Ripon were about to play a major part in the chronicle of the Great War. Command depots had been established everywhere and at Ripon, the centre for the Northern Command, there were Ripon North (1), Ripon North (2) and Ripon South, with a total accommodation of twenty-four officers and 12,000 men. We know of life at these camps, where the Pals battalions received their training after first steps taken in their own localities, from numerous memoirs. However, these camps were later to become 'convalescent camps', very different in nature from their purpose in 1915.

To gather some idea of how huge and impressive the camps were, a comparison of the land around Bishopton over to Studley Roger, to the west of the centre of Ripon, as shown on the 1911 ordnance survey map together with the available camp maps shows the transformation. Basically, great bustling towns were built; suburban sprawls on the edge of Ripon itself. On the 1911 map there is a string of tiny places, from Bishopton to High Birkby Nab and Hollin Head Wood, which is typically sparse, open agricultural land with copses, tracks and farms.

The North Camp that covered this in the war shows Bishopton Lodge nudging very close to lines of huts, bordered by three incinerators, the Garrison Theatre, a long stretch of railway sidings and then, within another half mile, more lines of huts, an isolation hospital and several more incinerators. To the east of Bishopton Lodge there were six large clusters of huts as far as the YMCA hut and Doublegates Lane, then nine more clusters of huts going to the extent of the camp with Green Lane at the north-east spot and the northern stretch of the River Laver in the central area, above the generating station and the power station. The overall extent of this camp was about 1.5 miles by 2 miles.

Memoirs from the ranks of the new recruits as well as from the seasoned professionals who knew Ripon are many and varied. There can be few sharper contrasts in the history of the camps than that at Studley Royal, as it was described in mid-Victorian times and as it was when transformed for military habitation. In 1875, the author wrote:

> After passing through the village of Studley, and arriving at the park lodge, the eye is restrained from excursion into the woodlands by a noble avenue of limes, above a mile in length, that guides our path and directs the eye to the church... the eye, that will be gladdened by nothing but nature, naked and unadorned, now appears joyfully through the thicket on an irregular pool...

By comparison, we have this account from a soldier, Private Tony Miller: 'I joined the signallers because I thought I'd get out of drilling and guard duty, and I did. Instead of doing a lot of guard duty we were learning the signals... We used to have rolls of wire to hug around and we used to have Morse code flags...' He also adds a touch of dark humour: '... we used to have sacks hung between posts and we used to charge these sacks and jab 'em with a bayonet... I thought if I were to miss these particular sacks in the charge and stab somebody, it'd be awkward...'

Naturally, organization was not always impressive, as a man commented in his notebook:

> At last, we reached camp. The huts were all that could be desired, but something had gone wrong with the commissary department and there was not a thing for us to eat when we arrived. Many of the fellows broke camp and made their way to a nearby village and to inns. About three hours later those who stayed hopefully and faithfully in camp received an issue of tea, bread and jam.'

He also summed up the training: 'Forming fours, route marching, applying bandages, physical jerks, polishing buttons and kit inspections etc.'

Kitchener had approved the plans for a camp at Ripon, with the aim of having one working by April. There was to be accommodation for over 30,000 men. The problem was that such a massive establishment would create local difficulties of all kinds. This was explained at a meeting in London to create a string of girls' patriotic clubs across the land in March. Lady Frances Balfour gave a speech, followed by Emily Kinnard who put her finger on the problem, referring to 'a great enthusiasm for khaki' and expanding on that with the following words, as reported in *The Times*:

> A great number of troops would be drafted into places where formerly there were not enough men to go round, and the girls would see the prospect of nice engagements resulting, or else, as in Ripon, where 14,000 troops had been drafted into a town of 8,000 people, the soldiers would crowd the population uncomfortably and have no place for the young girls to go of an evening.

The reasoning behind the planning of the training camps of such sheer massive size was that it made sense for a division, which was a block of fighting men within a battle order and a campaign, to train as well as fight together. Three infantry brigades constituted a division and each brigade had four battalions, so the New Army fitted in with the overall structure; men coming from various locations to meet and work with the other constituents of their division.

In practical terms, as the camps were made across the country, the huts had to be made to take around 800,000 troops. In Northern Command there were 200,000 men. As early as just a few weeks into the war, the Directorate of Fortifications and Works set about issuing orders, along with specifications, for the new huts which were named after Major Armstrong who commanded the Directorate. Armstrong's hut was to be 60ft long, 20ft wide and 10ft high. Each hut would hold thirty men. On top of this, there were other designated buildings such as sites for cooking, resources and supplies, guardroom and so on. Fir was used and also corrugated iron. Fortunately for those inside, asbestos was sampled and tested but then rejected.

The extent of the camps was indeed impressive. Ripon camps held around 15,000 men. In some places reservoirs had to be made, and power sources. There is no doubt that the logistics of planning and making the camps provide evidence of skilful and intelligent construction work. The army got some things right. The railway back-up continued through the war with, for instance, a line from Littlethorpe to one of the camps and later, from October 1917, an ambulance train for wounded men was shown to the public in Bower Road yard and as James Rogers has noted: 'Despite the very bad weather the train

NORTH EASTERN RAILWAY,

LEEDS "PALS" IN CAMP AT COLSTERDALE.

On SATURDAY, 31st OCTOBER, 1914,

An EXCURSION TRAIN will be run as under, to

HARROGATE
RIPON AND
MASHAM

	p.m.	To Harrogate	To Ripon	To Masham
		FARES THERE & BACK—THIRD CLASS.		
LEEDS (New Station) dep.	12 15	1/6	1/6	1/9
Holbeck ... ... "	12 20			
Headingley ... "	12 26			
Horsforth ... ... "	12 33			
HARROGATE ... "	1 0	—	1/6	1/6

RETURN ARRANGEMENTS THE SAME DAY AS FOLLOW:

MASHAM	dep.	8 30 p.m.
RIPON	"	8 52 "
HARROGATE	"	9 15 "

The Company reserve the right to cancel the train without notice if it should be necessary to do so.

NO LUGGAGE allowed. CHILDREN over 3 and under 12 years, half-fares.
TICKETS are not transferable;
are only available to and from stations for which issued and by excursion trains in both directions;
are not available for intermediate stations;
must be obtained before travelling or full ordinary fare will be charged;
are issued subject to General conditions and regulations specified in the Company's current time tables.

TICKETS, BILLS, and all particulars can also be obtained as under:—
From LEEDS ... { N.E.R. COMPANY'S CITY OFFICE, 12, Commercial Street.
Messrs. THOMAS COOK & SON, 55, Boar Lane.

For further information respecting this Excursion, apply to the Local Passenger Agent, Leeds (Tel. No. 4026); or to the Central Excursion Office, York (Tel. No. 264).

A notice showing the rail routes to the camps. (Author's own) attracted 2,551 visitors who paid, to the Red Cross, £145 0s 6d in admission charges.' Attendance at special exhibitions raised money very successfully, as Rogers adds that 'The previous April an egg and poultry demonstration train had attracted 1,360 people to Harrogate station.'

However, the locals were not happy. All those men thrown together, with a heady mix of camaraderie and a sense of adventure, was a recipe for chaos. The main element was, as usual, drink. Pub visits were banned until six in the evening, and of course there was always the YMCA. The authorities hoped that smiling faces and soft drinks would be a substitute for the wilder aspects of free time. In addition, there was a view that hard work would subdue the spirits and bring more sleep and rest; the diaries of some of the soldiers there do paint a picture of an uneasy mix of physical jerks and free time. For instance, in David Raw's book on the Bradford Pals, he quotes Herbert Taylor's diary and we have entries such as these:

> 19 Physical drill 6.45. Easy morning. Canteen corporal at 12
>   Company left at 3.00.
> 20 Did nothing all day. Company returned at 3.30. Lecture by
>   Captain Davis...
> 21 Musketry all morning and afternoon.
> 22 Brigade route march over eighteen miles by Brimham Rocks.

The basic regime of the camps, as conceived by the War Office, was to have bayonet and shooting training, recreation, consultation with medical staff and gymnasium exercises, with a fundamental progression of *esprit de corps* and inculcation of the right military mindset, rooted in discipline and teamwork. Camps generally were not exactly liked or celebrated. Herbert Read of the Green Howards wrote in his diary:

> I came to this dreadful place a week ago. The Medical Board gave me light duty – but they don't understand the term here... all the time the same monotonous work – shouting oneself hoarse, trying to initiate remarkably dense recruits into the mysteries of 'forming fours' etc. I think I shall flee to the Front for a little peace at the earliest opportunity.

However, across the whole country there were problems with the effects of leisure time on civilian localities. In March one reporter informed the public of a ban on officers visiting night clubs. The police official he spoke to told him 'One night club has already put up a notice to the effect that officers in uniform are not admitted, while another has issued a notification that officers and soldiers can only be admitted if wearing correct uniform.' There was, at this stage in the training, a fair amount of leisure time and as well as the Garrison Theatre being on the South Camp (as will be described later, when 1918 is reached) but of course there were all kinds of entertainment around the area, stretching from various places between north Leeds and the Harrogate and Knaresborough area to other village locations around Ripon. There was a film theatre at Wetherby, for instance, that opened in April 1915 and known as the Raby. A centenary celebration of the theatre in the *Advertiser* in April 2015 pointed out that it later became known as the Rodney and, of course, the fare for the war generation would have been such material as comedy shorts from the era of silent film.

The working of the camps was also a major challenge for the railways. The Great Northern Railway was central to the shuttling of troops up to Ripon and Harrogate. The line started at King's Cross and ran up to Shaftholme Junction, south of York. For wartime goods traffic as well, the line was very important. One historian has calculated that the number of wagons operated by the Great Northern working north and south between August 1914 and the Armistice was around 3 million.

The postcard images of that era give a clear idea of what the stations on the route from Leeds to Ripon and beyond were like at the time. One picture shows Cross Gates (which Harrogate women working in the Barnbow munitions factory would use to and from work) and it was a very attractive, well-kept place with shrubs in large planters and plenty of staff in attendance. The station would have also served routes to York, Selby and the East Coast.

Edwin Pratt, writing about the line in 1921 when memory was fresh, explained the rail network as it affected the northern camps:

> The Great Northern was also much concerned in the heavy traffic passing between London and the large camps at Ripon, Catterick, Clipstone and elsewhere in the Northern Command.

The proportion of servicemen in uniform carried on the Great Northern was about 60% as against 40% of civilians, and special steps had to be taken to ensure the provision of a maximum of possible space for passengers.

The line was also busy in the southerly direction, carrying Belgian refugees down to Alexandra Palace where they were dispersed to various homes. The same route was also later used for German prisoners of war being returned home.

Special trains were always provided, of course, in extreme situations and often staff had to be moved up north to Yorkshire from London. One dramatic and fateful instance of this was that of Lord Kitchener, bound north to board HMS *Hampshire* on which journey he would drown in 1916. Apparently, a message arrived for him from the Foreign Office shortly after his departure from King's Cross. A special was quickly arranged and this train passed the 156-mile post after a journey of 149 minutes. Kitchener waited briefly at York and caught the special, which took him on to his doomed sea journey.

In complete contrast, for the Ripon camps specials were put on at a cost of 1s 6d from Leeds to Ripon, as in the example of the excursion train provided on 31 October 1914 taking Leeds Pals from their home town to Harrogate and Ripon and as far as Masham.

A survey of these logistics at the camps supports Colette Hooper's assertion that the war was to transform the railway, just as much as the railway transformed the war: 'Railways were influencing military strategy before a shot was fired. They influenced where the war was fought, and helped entrench the stalemate... as total war extended its reach ever further, Britain's powerful rail industry was forced to make changes that ultimately altered the course of our railway history.'

It didn't take long for the various organizations at home to adapt hospitals ready to accept the wounded Tommies or for places such as stately homes to be used for that purpose. Even Blenheim Palace's library was converted for hospital use. The demands on the Voluntary Aid Detachment (VAD) nurses and on the amateurs who volunteered were going to be very great indeed. The VAD nurses usually were offered a probation period of one month and were given a small uniform allowance; a number of basic skills were necessary and the application forms listed these: skills such as writing legibly when filling in forms! The age range was 23 to 48 for foreign service and 21 to 48 for home service. Some professionals, after the war, saw the limitations of all this and recommended that nurses in the future be trained by the Territorial Army, but the invaluable contribution made by VAD nurses in the war cannot be overestimated.

Harrogate was going to be an important part of this medical work, being already a place renowned for cures, for treatment of invalids and for convalescence. We have some idea what it was like to work in such a place from the diary of Nurse de Trafford at Moor Park Military Hospital. At one stage she wrote about the whole process that mass arrivals entailed, including this very telling passage:

> The same night they arrive, we give them cards to address to their nearest relative –saying that they have got here... They are usually dead tired and fall asleep. Some of the surgeons come round... but the first dressings are usually done next morning as most of them have been done on the hospital ship – those first dressings, they are a sad sight – gauze soaked through with blood is peeled off the wound...

Harrogate was destined to be the kind of place that dealt with this kind of thing all through the war and beyond. The so-called auxiliary hospitals burgeoned. Tolkien, for instance, already mentioned, attended the Furness auxiliary hospital, and from letters and scraps of memories we can assemble a general overview of such places. There are even photos, of course, showing the large, airy rooms adapted as hospital wards. The foundation of all the care and treatment at these hospitals was fresh air, bed-rest, a pleasant atmosphere and the utmost cleanliness in bandaging and supervision of all kinds of wounds. Of course, the distinction between 'medical' and 'physical' cases mentioned by nurses hints at the special problems encountered in what Wilfred Owen ironically called 'Mental cases'. In other words, 'shellshock', or neurasthenia as it was called, provided a particularly challenging kind of work.

In September of that year, in this context of caring for the wounded, one of the most remarkable stories from Harrogate in the war was to begin. It concerns a woman who figures in her niece's memoirs like this:

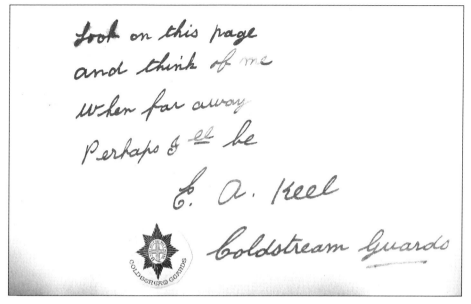

look on this page
and think of me
when far away
Perhaps I *ll* be

C. A. Keel

Coldstream Guards

An entry from a hospital nurse's autograph book. (Author's own)

> In April a yacht belonging to the Russian Black Sea squadron
> was sent to the Piraeus to take us to the Crimea. My mother's
> sister, her husband Grand Duke George, since assassinated, and
> their children went with me to Constantinople, where we stayed
> two days. It seemed to me the most beautiful city I had ever seen;
> I remember it as almost fairylike.

That was written by the Grand Duchess Marie, and her aunt, properly
referred to as Princess Maria of Greece and Denmark, was to become
known in Harrogate as the Grand Duchess George.

She was stranded in the town when war broke out but in 1910 she
had come to Harrogate, largely because her daughter Xenia was ill and
the town was recommended, as was so often the case, as a place for a
curative experience. The royal family returned again and again. She
married her maternal cousin, Grand Duke George, in 1900 and by the
time they came to Harrogate in the pre-war years, she had two
daughters, Nina and Xenia.

However, the last thing she did on finding herself adrift in a foreign country was to kick her heels and look for ways to fill the time. In September she set about creating a hospital for the wounded. In her diary when war was announced she had written 'Feel completely crushed and anxious… a real hell of a position. May God have pity on His world.'

The ideal of service filled her being, as was the case with so many women in 1914. Her actions are summed up by Tennyson's words 'Something of noble note may yet be done.' Indeed, she set about recruiting suitably qualified medics for her hospital and a private house was transformed into a twelve-bed hospital. As Tom Rowley has noted: 'In the early days, not everything went to plan. The first matron was an alcoholic. Then the War Office objected to the hospital, resenting the dominance of a foreigner. A letter from the King soon overcame their concerns.'

The story of how this developed is not only touching but splendidly heartening, given the surge of invalids returning home for care around Harrogate and Ripon. The evidence shows that she and her staff formed a special bond of affection and care for their charges. She even bought a blue outfit for the patients and they were termed her 'boys in blue'.

Malcolm Neesam, who presented a special celebration of Duchess George's work at the Harrogate Festival in 2014, has said that the first arrivals for treatment were greeted on the station platform and treated with a sense of elation and welcome. What about the standard of care? Mr Neesam said: 'They were highly qualified in the science of their day... we would probably find it primitive and frightening but it was better than nothing.'

After the hospital came a convalescent home. That was a major development of Ripon and Harrogate, almost providing the main template for their war experience; 1914 brought the training camps and hospitals, and later in the conflict the dispersal camps and convalescent homes took prominence.

After the war, Grand Duchess George moved to Rome. She married Admiral Pericles Ioannides and she died in 1940 in Athens. However, Harrogate persisted as a special place in her heart. A writer went to see her in Rome and he reported that the walls were covered with pictures: 'There were countless framed photographs... of her hospitals in

Harrogate, of groups of wounded Tommies, and grateful letters sent to her. It was her shrine. I was too moved to speak,' he wrote.

Today she is still remembered in Harrogate by the memorial on the edge of the Stray and also thanks to the good work of Malcolm Neesam who wrote the show about her *That Most Gracious and Noble Lady*, and to the Pump Room Museum who featured her in their major exhibition of 2014.

The last months of 1914 brought tales of what was happening in France but there was also the visible proof of upheaval with refugees and casualties. One man wrote: 'This chilly, misty evening, it is my privilege to entertain the Vandenberger family – or rather, what remains of the Vandenberger family – in a corner of the refreshment rooms of Waterloo station.' That scenario was all too common. Around Harrogate, plenty was being done for the Belgian refugees. The Belgian Relief Fund was up and running with £250 being collected by the end of the year, along with £448 for the Distress Fund. One press report gave more details about the help being provided:

> Accommodation for the Belgian refugees has been most generously provided, and the first little company sent from headquarters arrived on Thursday night. A comfortable and spacious house, St John's Lodge, near Bond End, has been given by Miss Shaw, who has offered it rent free for a year... A great many people in the town are giving sums up to 2s 6d a week to help with the upkeep of the home. Furniture has been so readily given and lent that there is already sufficient to furnish two houses instead of one. Here is an opportunity for another kind sympathiser to add to this record of golden deeds. The extra furniture is waiting. Who will offer another house for a second pitiful little band of grief-stricken refugees from brave little Belgium...

Over in France there were plenty of sad stories of death and suffering in the last months of the year. One particular death – that of Captain Thomas Cecil de Trafford – represents one of the most poignant instances of loss and a young life cut down. Thomas was born in 1881 and was originally regarded as a good recruit for the navy, but his eyesight was not adequately acute. He attended Stonyhurst College and

Captain Thomas Cecil de Trafford. (Stonyhurst Great War Archive)

did very well at sports, leaving that college in 1899 to study engineering. He was then gazetted to the Royal Fusiliers and saw service abroad before being made captain in 1910. Then, in September 1914, as the war was fresh and challenging all military men, he made his Harrogate connection by marrying Freya, daughter of Sir Joseph Radcliffe of Rudding.

On 11 November he was reported missing after taking part in the disastrous fight at Nonne Bosschen (Nun's Copse) in the First Battle of Ypres. In this battle, two of the best German outfits had led the advance: the Prussian Guards and the 4th Division. Their aim was to break the British lines and make for their main objective of Hooge. They met the British at the Menin Road, with Nun's Copse as the focus. Thomas de Trafford was involved in this and the fight lasted all day. Only by gathering all kinds of ancillary men, including cooks and pioneers, did the British succeed in a holding operation.

Of course, the family at Rudding Park had a long and tortuous wait. Thomas was missing, presumed dead, and that was indeed the case. His brother Henry had already been killed in September 1914. Rudding Park had been bought by the Radcliffes back in 1824 and Sir Joseph Edward, who died in 1949, felt a pall of gloom over the place on hearing the sad news from France about Thomas Cecil. However, his widow Freya did marry again.

A look at the Stonyhurst College Great War archive very powerfully conveys how many excellent young men from their ranks gave their lives in the war. Thomas was one of the elite, highly-regarded, from a wealthy family and of high status. In complete contrast there were countless other deaths but, ironically, as death has no respect for status, many of the ordinary working lads in the new battalions died with some kind of record. Such was the case with Fred Tucker from Harrogate, whose father received a note from Fred's sergeant in which there are words that his father would have valued as there was a crumb of comfort in that 'He was killed absolutely instantaneously, as he was lying so peacefully with a beautiful smile on his face. He was laid to rest with all the other boys we left there.'

Mr Tucker at least knew his son's final resting place. For the Radcliffes, their young bridegroom was missing, presumed dead, and the agony went on.

CHAPTER 2

1915
The Home Front War
Effort and Trench Warfare

The year 1915 was to be the phase of the war in which, after the massive shock of large-scale losses at the front and a consequent stalemate, with armies digging in and creating an impasse, now it was in the German mind that technology was needed to make progress. That was to mean gas, more lethal weaponry and an increasing attitude that the aim of annihilation of the enemy was paramount.

At home, the first day of the New Year brought shocking news for the Reverend Slingsby of Scriven Park, Knaresborough. His son, midshipman John, was on board HMS *Formidable* when she was hit by two torpedoes in the Channel. He was killed, at just 16 years of age. *Formidable* had joined the 5th Battle Squadron in 1912 after serving in the Mediterranean and she was only the second British battleship to be destroyed in the U-boat war. The development of genealogy has brought a definite interest in the surname Slingsby and there were very many men called Slingsby who died in the war, one of the most poignant deaths being that of Lance Corporal Thomas Slingsby of the East Yorkshire Regiment who was shot by a female sniper just a few weeks before he was due to marry his fiancée, Mary Longden.

By the end of 1914 the British army had lost 90,000 officers and men in the first five months of combat. However, there had been reserve forces available: there was plenty of manpower in the reserve battalions, almost 150,000 in fact. There were various other forces too, in a number of reserve categories. Consequently, volunteers did not participate in the action on the Western Front or in the east until halfway through 1915, in most cases. More than one million men had responded to Kitchener's call for enlistment. The challenges of the coming year, therefore, had troops in great numbers waiting to meet them.

In the pages of the *Harrogate Herald*, however, in spite of the horrors of war in the field, Breare worked hard to maintain morale by doing two important things: he communicated good humour and he made the material effects of the war familiar. He seemed to realize that if he kept on talking about actual individuals, with names and addresses and accounts of how they spoke and what they wore, then the accoutrements of military life would become everyday matters, close to home in every sense.

Just a few weeks into the year, for instance, he wrote about a German helmet:

> The first German helmet reached Harrogate on Friday. It was sent from France by Dick Whitehead, whose wife despatched it to the *Herald* office to be photographed and exhibited in the window. It had been worn by one of the Landsturm [militia or reserves], who was shot in the back of the head. The hole caused by the bullet is plainly discernible. The helmets are heavy, uncomfortable things; for show rather than for comfortable service, we all think.

Breare liked his little joke as well. After all, this was the war depicted in satirical postcards produced by Bruce Bairnsfather and of comic songs about Tommies and trenches. Breare's contribution, to crack the faces of Harrogate folk over breakfast, was as follows:

> It is possibly an old tale revived, but the story goes that one of the officers of a present Harrogate contingent was drilling his men on the Stray. His commands are given in a deep voice that 'bays'. He barks his orders in the regulation form. 'Stand at ease!' The men stood easy – a pause. A deep-mouthed dog barked twice, 'bow-wow' – the men formed fours.

When the urgent need for more munitions became evident during this year, the politicians must have regretted the fact that nothing very much had been done in response to the reports produced by the Women's Industrial Council, which had been advocating better working conditions and training for women in factories, and in particular for women in domestic industry such as tinplate badge-making (for which, in a war, there was a constant demand). The Council's Technical Training Committee, in 1900, for instance, had pointed out the necessity of describing exactly what training, if any, was given to girls 'of the industrial class' at technical institutes and also it had set out to discover which skilled trades for women would benefit from proper industrial training. Of course, war was not foremost in people's minds in 1900, but the future had proved the council right in insisting that one day women would be needed in the metal industries in rather greater numbers and in a wider range of skilled jobs.

A popular song of the war, *Sister Susie's Sewing Shirts for Soldiers*, has fun at the expense of women who were filling in for the men in any number of occupations but it doesn't come near the reality, especially when we consider the munitions factories. The recruiting for shell factory jobs echoed the men's enlistment in some ways. They were also up against male resentment. A worker called Elsa Thomas commented on this: 'They didn't want to show us their livelihood: they knew it was their livelihood. Women were coming in. They were going to cut the wages... They didn't say it to me, but you had that feeling you were going to take a man's wage from him.'

There were great risks involved in munitions work and several regions had their tales of horrendous accidents, but one of the worst happened not so far from Harrogate. This was at the Barnbow factory where the poor munitionettes, as they were called, experienced a terrible horror in 1916 (see Chapter Three for details). The whole physical atmosphere of the places was clearly harmful and repugnant and everyone knew the risks.

The martial events of the year began with Yorkshire figuring prominently in the war news, and it was nothing to do with the Western Front. The Zeppelins attacked the east coast: Hull, Scarborough and Hartlepool were bombed, following a first wave lower down at Great Yarmouth and King's Lynn. To folk in Ripon and Harrogate, bombs in Scarborough seemed very close and so the war was coming to the home

A typical workshop during shell production. (Author's own)

front rather more directly than in the last months of 1914 when the soldiers had gathered and gone off to camp.

There were also other notably unpleasant and worrying effects of the war becoming more apparent as the months passed, such as xenophobia. Anti-German feeling was intensifying throughout the 1914–15 period and matters were made much worse by the sinking of the *Lusitania* in May after she had sailed from Liverpool. The outrage after this was savage and often irrational. Civilians on board had perished after the vessel was torpedoed by a U-boat and gangs around Liverpool beat up anyone who might be considered to be German, including anyone with an un-English and vaguely European name. Establishments with German-sounding names were also prime targets. In Leeds and Bradford, however, places with significant German and Jewish populations (in which names sounding Germanic would have made people vulnerable) there was little open trouble. Some of the irrational fear and hatred had the most terrible effects, as explained in

A drawing showing the German U-boat and its target ship, the Lusitania. *(The Great War in Europe)*

a letter to *The Times* in 2015 from Michael Myer, who wrote: 'My grandfather was not German. He was a Lithuanian Jew, but it did him no good trying to tell his neighbours that as they smashed up his shop. His name happened to be Schneiderman.'

A Czech gentleman wrote, anonymously, to the *Spectator* in April, explaining something at the very heart of this paranoia about foreigners. He wrote: 'An invisible, yet for all that quite tangible, barrier seems to have arisen around me. I shrink from meeting you lest I be taken for a spy.' His point was that he had felt English, and had been accepted as English, until the wartime fears spread the irrational behaviour he could see around him.

The issue of men in the ranks who came from German families was not so rare in Yorkshire: after all, there had been large waves of German immigrants throughout the nineteenth century to Bradford, Leeds and many other Yorkshire towns. The usual strategy was to adopt an English name, as was the case with the Steinthal brothers. Paul Steinthal joined the Royal Artillery as a Major Paul Petrie, and his brother Francis also took the name of Petrie.

There was nothing new about that xenophobia either. Mill girl Maggie Newbury recalled in her autobiography, referring to autumn 1914: 'We were soon to see some of the uglier aspects of war, when gangs of hooligans went and broke windows of shops owned by Germans. These shopkeepers were in the main good honest people who had served us well with their pork shops and delicatessens.'

There is a particularly ironic twist to the topic of Germans being in Harrogate and the general xenophobia of 1915. Malcolm Neesam refers to a German connection in his book on the Majestic Hotel:

The originator of the Anglo-German motor tour of Great Britain was Prince Henry of Prussia, brother to the German Emperor, Wilhelm II. It was Prince Henry's belief that some of the difficulties between the two nations were caused by unfamiliarity, and that this could be countered by motor tours in each country. In July, 1911 the Anglo-German motor car tour of Great Britain selected Harrogate as the half-way point of their rally... the Hotel Majestic naturally figured as their principal address. Trophies for the rally were provided by Prince Henry...

He adds that 'Townsfolk gathered on Leeds Road on 12 July. The Conan Doyles were in the Majestic and decamped to the Grand...'

However, in an interesting footnote to the topic, the story of Professor Schuddekopf, an academic at Leeds University, highlights the special nature of Harrogate in this context. In the violent atmosphere of the anti-German feeling in 1915, Schuddekopf, whose son had enlisted in the Leeds Rifles, made a discreet request to the high command that his son be sent anywhere except the Western Front as he would be potentially facing his own relatives in battle. The news of this led to a campaign to sack Schuddekopf, and Frank Finlay explained in his account of the story: 'The Home Secretary explained that it implied nothing to his discredit and compassionately endorsed the suggestion that he withdraw on an extended leave of absence to the spa town of Harrogate, which promised respite and the distractions of a renowned musical scene.' Once again, as was so often the case, the town was defined (and successful) as the location for renewal, therapy and peace.

On the credit side, very positive steps were being taken on the home front around the Harrogate area in terms of support and provision of hospital work. Women were joining the VAD and other nursing organizations and there was also a desperate need for hospital supply depots. Private individuals played an important part in this, such as Mrs Greenwood of Swarcliffe, Birstwith, and further afield in Kirkbymoorside, Mrs Shaw-Hellier of Welburn Manor. These were crucially important in the supply system as basic hospital materials were always needed and as the war went on, all possible sources of materials were used, even down to invalided soldiers gathering sphagnum moss for use in dressings. Fortunately, England's extensive railway network was available to gather and transport materials from obscure corners of the shires out to the front.

Researchers have to dig long and hard into archives for details of the work done by individual women across the whole spectrum of work in the war, but one fruitful way to understand this is to look at some of the work undertaken by the girls from St George's School for Girls in Edinburgh as this was where Miss G.M. Wilson, the Welfare Superintendent at the Ripon camps, was schooled. She worked in Ripon for ten months, for the NACB (the National Army Catering Board), and a cross-section of the work done by her schoolfellows gives this list: cook; canteen work; fruit-farming; Red Cross rest-room work; hospital dispensary; Scottish Churches hut, France; Women's Legion motor driver; teacher of French to men of the 16th Battalion, Royal Scots; and War Dressing Association attachment. Miss Wilson's work in catering for the men at the Ripon camps was absolutely essential, as an army does indeed march on its stomach. The point here is that educated women flocked to all available work and Ripon, as a massive focus for soldiery, saw this variety of workers during the war years.

There was also the work of the Catholic Women's League, which provided a service alongside the YMCA. They provided a 'Mother hut' at Studley; as with the YMCA, the Catholic Women's League (CWL) had created huts across the war zones. The league had been founded in Brighton in 1906 and four years later there was a meeting of the International Union of Catholic Women's Leagues in Brussels, dealing with such topics as female education and working conditions. Just before the war, their conference was held in London. Margaret Fletcher, the driving force behind the organization, had her resources ready when war broke out.

Only a few weeks into the war, there was already a team of twenty-two trained nurses in Belgium. What followed, as the enterprise expanded, was work in all areas where refugees were found and where relief was needed. By early 1915 the CWL had given the huge sum of £10,408 to a range of wartime needs. Everything had started with a call for a hut at Boulogne and one was made; then followed other huts at home, starting with one installed at St Peter's Hall, Westminster. It was a scheme subject to a high demand and a committee was formed in 1917 to supervise the running of the provision.

The West Riding Branch then opened a hut and a chapel at Studley Roger, to handle the needs of the two camps. As the author of a memorial feature for the CWL wrote in 2014: 'It was staffed by CWL members who worked round the clock to provide over a thousand meals a day for the men who camped there.' This became known as the 'English Mother Hut.' It was sold after the war and a plinth placed there in memory of the hut and the people who kept it going.

Just a few years after the war, the CWL Leeds Branch made their annual pilgrimage to the memorial. The *Tablet* reported: 'The base of the crucifix was decorated with flowers given by the wives of soldiers living on the camp, and the Harrogate Girls' Club again sent a beautiful wreath. Many friends joined the pilgrimage, amongst them being those from Studley Roger who were close neighbours of the hut during the war.'

Harrogate itself featured in a national newspaper, due to its being defined as a centre for invalids. The writer took up this theme and then went deeper: 'To those who have never been there, the mention of Harrogate may call up a scene of elderly folk – sallow from stomach and liver troubles... hobbling on sticks or crutches or wheeled about in bath chairs...' The contrast is sharp: 'Such a picture of Harrogate as a resort of invalids is quite erroneous. For most visitors the abiding memory of Harrogate is that of a place of infectious gaiety... The place has never been more crowded than it is this season.'

Following that overall view, the author notes what the war was doing to the town:

But the war has thrown its shadow over Harrogate, as over all holiday resorts. Not that anyone appears to want to... The more dark the outlook, the brighter must shine the star of duty through the gloom. That appears to be the uplifting mood of the throng of visitors at Harrogate. So the old merry-making and frivolity of the place are gone... The visitors seem as intent as ever on following the discipline of 'the cure' with strict regularity.

The writer then turns the notes on duty and resolution to the spirit of the war effort: 'Visitors are now more disposed to discuss the disease of the Commonwealth; and whether or not they agree that National Service will prove an efficacious medicine, they all acknowledge that everything must be subordinate to the supreme task of saving the state.'

Across the Channel, the Pals battalions were beginning to see action by May. It was in that month and the following months that many of these men participated in fighting, after long months of training and life in huts in open spaces. Many of the Ripon-based men were at the front by May. The attitudes of the people at home were fixed on giving all the help they could to their Tommies. One piece of typical good-feeling propaganda explains the attitude of humour and stoicism; a supposed officer (in the paper) wrote a general letter to the civvies, saying:

> Your parcel of shortbread arrived last night. We will have some great 'teas' while it lasts. As regards the financial matter – don't send any money here. I can always get money from a carefully-well-groomed gentleman called the divisional cashier... there is little need to buy and when a rich country feeds its soldiers so well...

The fact was that by the end of 1914, Britain had suffered around 89,000 casualties and over 1 million men had enlisted by that Christmas. The Battle of Neuve Chapelle in March had set the tone of what was to follow but late April through to the end of May showed how the extremes of trench warfare could go; notably with the first use of poison gas, chlorine, which would later be followed by the even more deadly phosgene. When this second Ypres scrap was over, there were 60,000 men lost from the allied ranks. It must be significant that, in March, war correspondents were banned from the front. The *Spectator* reported: 'The exclusion of war correspondents from the firing line has greatly reduced the volume of unofficial news available for the enlightenment of the general public. What remains, however, has to run the gauntlet of the censorship. How some of it manages to get through is a mystery.'

Neuve Chapelle in March of that year generated some outstanding military experience, as one would expect, bearing in mind that British

*Clearing station: a drawing from the regimental history of the West Riding
Territorials. (Harrogate Central Library)*

casualties in that action were around 11,600. Sir John French wanted Neuve Chapelle taken and the Germans did as they usually did, bringing a sustained mass of shellfire to 'flatten out' the opposition. However, the allies got in first this time. The first British assault was against the arm of the enemy commanded by Crown Prince Rupprecht and an account written not long after the events describes what happened:

> Hell opened its mouth and belched forth fire and brimstone. The wind was torn, the ear pierced by the rush and roar of high explosives and shrapnel shells. A wall of fire fell upon the German trenches, and the men in them were dazed... Many went mad with horror... the hail of shell continued, the gunners working with a grim joy as they marked how, under the bombardment from their huge howitzers firing lyddite, the enemy's trenches fell in... Meantime, the troops who were to make the charge waited....

These were the men of five brigades of the 8th Division. They dashed at the German trenches and mostly this was a smooth operation but one – 23 Brigade – found that the wires in front of them were uncut and this made them vulnerable when trying to get through. However, later, when the advance was resumed, things went wrong. Then after 12 March, the Germans brought in considerable reinforcements. Nevertheless, counter-attacks proved effective and the result was advantageous to the allies. Yet, and this is a word backed up by staggering facts, the British losses included 190 officers and 2,337 men, with a further 8,000 or more wounded.

Sir Douglas Haig sent an Order of the Day message to Haig and the 1st Army: 'I am anxious to express to you my warmest appreciation of the skilful manner in which you have carried out your orders, and my fervent and most heartfelt appreciation of the magnificent gallantry and devoted, tenacious courage displayed by all ranks whom you have ably led to success...'

Some of the men who were at Neuve Chapelle had their tales inevitably filtered into Breare's columns. Once again, he managed to make the moment a massive slice of triumphant patriotic cheer, especially when he printed the following letter from Corporal George Petty:

Well, now for a little news. You will, of course, have heard about our grand victory at Neuve Chapelle. What an experience! I am afraid we lost a lot of good men, but what must the German losses have been. Good gracious! They were lying in heaps all over the place. Our artillery opened the ball... Germans kept coming out in batches and holding their hands up, surrendering, and we noticed an incident just in front of us, coming out to give themselves up, and two or three men in a regiment in front of us got out of their trench, and advanced to bring them in, but our chaps were shot dead instantly... we were wild, and vowed each in his own picturesque way what would happen to them...

Of course, Harrogate men died in the battle, one of them being Lance Corporal George Lund, whose brother Walter was to die in May 1917. The *Herald* reported that a comrade had written to George's mother, who lived on Franklin Road:

I know, Mrs Lund, you will miss him, but you will not miss him more than I do. We have got lots of burial grounds round this part; some graves have got 30 or 40 bodies in... Your son has a grave to himself, so anything you wish doing to it I will be only too pleased to do...

Early in the year – February and March – Russia, allies of Britain, called for British involvement against the Turks (allied with Germany) and the challenge was an assault on the coast against Turkish defences at the Gallipoli peninsula. The campaign was a disaster, resulting in massive loss of life. The word 'Gallipoli' has always been one of the most doom-laden, desperately evocative words of all the Great War confrontations. Recently (in 2015) Gary Sheffield has challenged some of the assumptions about the fight, however. In an article outlining the assumptions, he concludes:

For the ordinary soldier the campaign was bereft of glory and romance. Instead there were primitive trenches that were so close to the beaches that even in rear areas it was impossible ever to be completely free of danger, vermin, dust that got into food and tea and the ever-present flies...

Cuts, sores and insect bites easily became infected (the cause of death of the poet Rupert Brooke, for instance). Basically, British and ANZAC troops were against guns on a higher position and were trapped on the deadly beaches.

Present at Gallipoli was Harrogate man Arthur Pigg, born in 1893. He was born on Teesside, but the family moved to Harrogate and Arthur enlisted in the West Yorkshire Regiment in 1914. In researching Arthur's life, his great-nephew was informed by historian Andrew Jackson that Arthur was with the 9th battalion, which left Liverpool for Gallipoli in July that year. It was one of Kitchener's battalions and the men participated in the fateful landings at Suvla Bay. After that, the men went to Egypt and then France. His medals index card shows that Arthur served in those places. His fate was an eventual breakdown and the year of his death is unknown.

At Suvla, as Gary Sheffield writes, he would have avoided the worst of the confrontation with the Turks as the main landing was at Anzac Cove, but the casualties were staggering: 'The Australians had the second highest casualties... The figures for Allied killed and wounded make sobering reading. The British suffered 70,700 casualties...'

In another more distant arena in the great theatre of war, this time in India at Hafiz Kor on the North-West Frontier, Harrogate man Charles Hull won the VC through rescuing an officer from certain death. To modern eyes, it may seem odd that there were wars going on in such distant places at the same time as the great battles in Europe, but the Indian army was facing tribal assaults by the Mohmands, Bunervals and Swatis in this year, and at Hafiz Kor 2,000 tribesmen attacked the troops of the Ist Peshawar Division. Hull was there as a blacksmith in support of the lines, but he certainly saw action. His VC citation reads:

> 1953 Private (Shoeing-Smith) Charles Hull, 21st Lancers: For most conspicuous bravery. When under fire of the enemy, who were within a few yards, he rescued Captain E.D. Learoyd, whose horse had been shot, by taking him up behind him and galloping into safety. Shoeing-Smith Hull acted entirely on his own initiative, and saved his officer's life at the imminent risk of his own.

Hull came home to Harrogate in 1919 and Breare, naturally, made a point of celebrating the man's achievements:

> Hull ... reached home on Monday night after being away some nine years. His arrival was totally unexpected by his family, as, though it was known late in the day that the ship in which he had crossed had docked at Portsmouth... the messages he had sent from the ship were delayed... the train, on its way to Ripon Dispersal Camp ran through Harrogate early on Monday morning... [the then] Corporal Hull looked the picture of health after the Indian campaign and has grown and filled out after nine years abroad...

Hull was also awarded the Croix de Guerre by the French. Captain Learoyd wrote and added to his letter of thanks this note: 'It would be in accordance with the fitness of things if the townspeople were given an opportunity of publicly welcoming Corporal Hull back to his native town.' He was duly welcomed back and on his return to 'Civvy Street' he became a constable in the Leeds City Police; in 1920 he married and settled down to a life of comparative peace.

It is easy to forget that there was a theatre of war out in India as the carnage grew in the trenches across Europe. At the same time that Hull was dealing with the tribes and winning his award, there was an ongoing fight in the Punjab. The Ghadar Party was active in wanting Home Rule and an end to being 'slaves of Empire'. Basically, as a pamphlet of the time explained, the Ghadar Party (mostly Sikhs) had 12,000 followers by 1914 and on the outbreak of war they saw the opportunity to strike. The pamphlet explained that '... it seemed that the only way to overthrow British rule was to bring about a revolt by the Indian Army.' There were large portions of the Indian army out fighting in France and so the revolutionaries saw a weak spot. However, they failed, and 'Scores were hanged, hundreds sentenced to long terms of imprisonment.'

Harrogate man Charles Hull's India was a perfect example of that tendency for a large-scale war to open up opportunities for restless minorities. He won his honour out on the periphery but nevertheless, he has a very special place in Harrogate history.

What about the ordinary men, by this time dying in great numbers over in France; what do we really know about them? Most are statistics, but sometimes some individuals are discovered and their story told with rather more than a few facts. One such case from 1915 has been revealed through family history work. The man in question is Lance Corporal Ronald Marshall, and Colin Waite investigated his story for the *Claro History* journal. What is of special interest here is that Marshall's story touches on that of a famous soldier of the war: poet John McCrae, who wrote the poem *In Flanders Fields*.

Colin Waite locates the focus of the tale at Boezinge, close to Ypres, at a dressing station. Marshall was there, in the very place where the famous poem was written. Colin Waite reports on the headstones and, after describing the scene, he writes that the stones are of the men 'mainly from the 49th West Riding and 38th Welsh Divisions, who died in 1915 and 1916... including Ronald Marshall, who is recorded on the Commonwealth War Graves Commission website as the "son of Mr and Mrs O. Marshall of 16, Regent Grove, Harrogate. Born York, remembered with honour."'

The poignant story of Ronald Marshall is that he was gassed and reported missing on 19 December 1915. The gas in question was phosgene and this was first used at that very time, superseding chlorine. As a defence, the small box respirator did offer some protection but that was not introduced until 1916. If Lance Corporal Marshall did have a gas mask, it would most likely have been a gas helmet, invented by Cluny MacPherson in July of this year; this was a canvas hood with a breathing-tube. Of course, the hard fact in Marshall's case is that it was not fitted in time. We know that these occurrences were tragically likely to happen from Wilfred Owen's famous poem *Dulce et Decorum Est*, in which we have the lines:

> Gas! Gas! Quick boys! – an ecstasy of fumbling,
> Fitting the clumsy helmets just in time;
> But someone still was yelling out and stumbling
> And flound'ring like a man in fire or lime...

As many have pointed out, Britain was slow to understand and deal with the gas attacks. L.F. Haber, writing in 1976, explained: 'The Allies, despite advance warning from agents and prisoners, were surprised by the Germans and unprotected against gas. They wanted to retaliate at once, but the necessary preparations took five months.' However, he also pointed out that 'taking the war as a whole and all the belligerents together, gas shells represented less than 5% of all ammunition fired in the Great War. For Germany the proportion was 6.4%, for Britain (owing to the continued use of cylinders) it was just over 2%.'

The advent of gas had been described in the papers from early on. In *The Times* on 9 April this year, a piece 'from an eye-witness' had this account: 'They prepare to asphyxiate our men if they advance by means of poison gas. The gas is contained under pressure in steel cylinders, and being of a heavy nature, will spread along the ground without being dissipated quickly.' Dr J.B. Haldane had been sent out to investigate the gas in this year and he travelled to the front line where he saw some of the Canadian casualties who were suffering from the effects of the new gas; he saw the men, struggling to breathe, their faces blue-tinged with cyanosis, and he also saw the autopsy on one who perished. He made it clear in his report that the severe bronchitis and damage to lung tissue were absolutely lethal and chances of survival were slim.

The story of Lance Corporal Marshall is part of a more prominent Harrogate story, as shown by a feature by John Sheehan in the *Advertiser*. Sheehan followed in the soldiers' footsteps as he went on a history trail in France, and he focuses on Colonel C.E. Wood who 'led his contingent of Harrogate men to the trenches....' Apparently the Harrogate men held up a sign showing how many German prisoners were in their hands after Loos. There was a German retaliation, the British trench was attacked and there was hand-to-hand fighting; eventually the Germans were rebuffed. Then, later, came the gas. Sheehan has traced the Tommies' lives, noting that, for instance, Norman Beech was a gents' outfitter who worked in Prospect Street. He notes that ten local men died during those few days, along with Marshall. John Sheehan went to the actual location of this terrible confrontation with gas and he wrote: 'To the right is the slight rise to the German trenches where the gas canisters were opened. On this ridge Norrie Beech planted his machine gun...'

The *Advertiser* feature includes photos of some of the men: Norman Beech, James Cahill, Francis Peacock, Ronald Marshall and Cecil Yates. The most striking aspect of the way in which the gas was used is made very clear by John Sheehan's account: it was the action it had of moving through the trenches at low level that was so lethal. The combination of the new gas and the machine guns stands out as a sure recipe for the rapid extinction of the heroic young men who encountered them.

One way to understand the sheer universality of the wartime events from the front is to look at the publications at home, produced within a certain atmosphere of people trying their best to maintain some sense of normality and routine. Hence, in *The Riponian*, the magazine of the Ripon Grammar School, for July this year we have listings of Old Riponians serving with the forces (a list filling three pages of the magazine), and also the lists of casualties and deaths. In July four ex-scholars were reported wounded, two had been taken prisoner and two had been killed, the latter being J.F. I'Anson, captain in the 1st Battalion West Yorks, and Richard Healey, acting engineer on the *Good Hope*, lost in action off Chile.

On a more heartening note, the same issue notes that an old boy had won the MC. This was 'Captain Mangin, E.B., who has received from the hands of His Majesty the King the decoration of the Military Cross for "Distinguished service in the Field" and he has also been Mentioned in Despatches.'

Without doubt, the Riponian old boys served their country across the whole span of the theatres of war embraced by the term 'global' as it was understood at the time, when people began to talk of a 'world war'. From the old boys lost at sea and on land, the spectrum goes from John Balfour Ireland, for instance, of the Black Watch, to the young officers who were cut down in arguably the most atrocious debacle of 1916 at the Somme.

The Riponians wrote from the front as well. One outstanding example is a very long and detailed letter – a complete memoir in itself – by Lieutenant A.F. Newton of the 2nd West Yorks. He had been asked by the editor to send some information and he responded with the sure hand of a professional reporter. His piece includes the minutiae of life in the dugouts, with a real documentary feel to the style:

Life in the trenches: The word 'trench' always appears to me somewhat of a misnomer as applied to the firing-lines of the armies engaged in the present conflict; for it implies a sort of

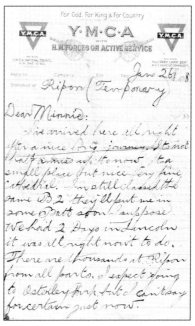

The cover of The Riponian *school magazine. (Ripon Grammar School)*

A letter home from Ripon Camp to Grimsby. Men from the Lincolnshire Regiment trained at Ripon before being sent out to the fight. (Author's collection)

ditch dug in the ground. The modern trench is nothing of the kind. It is dug down very little, if at all, but a parapet or breastwork of earth is thrown up in front, and built up with sandbags to a height of six feet or more... Also loop-holes are made in places for use by snipers during the daytime, but it is essential that these loop-holes should be well concealed...

The writer's literary training and taste come out when he turns to describing the locality: 'It is a piteous sight to see the ruined and deserted farms that are scattered all over the countryside... People at home cannot possibly realize what it is like to have war brought to one's very doors....'

Another casualty listed in the sad statistics of Ripon Grammar School reminds the reader that the war extended to Africa. This was

Robert Aslin, who was born in Ripon in 1887 and became a master mariner on HMS *Hyacinth*. The ship featured in what has become known as the Fight at Lubembe Point on 6 December of this year. The background involves British planned incursions into German-held territories in Africa. These had been established over thirty years earlier when the 'carving-up' of Africa by the European imperialist powers of Britain, Belgium, France and Germany had taken place.

In this December, the plan was that there would be a British advance from Uganda into lands then known as Kenya, Nyasaland and Northern Rhodesia; in step with this, Belgian forces were to move across from the Congo. In the first eighteen months of the war, Lake Victoria had been taken by British forces and now this needed to be reinforced and consolidated. Therefore, as was the usual practice ever since the Anglo-Zulu War of 1879, British sailors and marines were used on land as troops. The Royal Navy men were transported north by rail from Mombasa on the coast and they were joined by men from the Royal Naval Reserve cadres. On top of this, the 98th Infantry were also close by at the Lubembe peninsula.

This is where Robert Aslin enters the African chronicle of events, as he was on board the *Hyacinth*. The infantry had to be taken from a beach and the vessels *Winifred* and *Kavirondo* were in support of the action. These ships went in close to give covering fire as smaller boats evacuated men and supplies; however, there were German vessels against them and the *Hyacinth* was then brought in. Aslin, while trying to throw a line to a smaller boat, was shot and mortally wounded. Eventually all the small boats were towed to safety.

Robert Aslin lies in Entebbe European Cemetery and the only dubious element in his story is that, apparently, one report gives his vessel as the *Pegasus* but, as one writer has noted, that ship was scrapped in 1914.

The grave of Robert Aslin at Entebbe European Cemetery. (Greta Hills)

CHAPTER 3

1916
Meeting the Challenge –
Courage and Conscription

For people from all walks of life, the New Year was to bring home to everyone concerned in the war that it had escalated into massive proportions: losses had been great and everyone, at home and on active service, had been asked again and again to contribute, to grit their teeth and survive. The great maw of war demanded resources of every kind, from men's lives to basic provisions. As far as North Yorkshire was concerned, apart from manpower there was a high demand for something else that was available in abundance in that part of the country: wood.

Madeleine Bunting, in her book *The Plot*, explains this powerfully:

> In 1916 there were 2,000 miles of trenches on the western and eastern fronts, and the only weapon against the sea of mud was sawn timber. Tons of shuttering and duck-boards were needed to floor, wall and roof the trenches... Behind the lines, more timber was needed: huts were required to shelter troops and sleepers were needed for the network of light railways...

Between May 1917 and November 1918, the British army needed 5.7 million tons of planking and 7 million railway sleepers.

As the lists of casualties grew, another category of resource was in demand: the back-up services of nurses and drivers, general carers and other transport and provisions personnel. Among these, Harrogate has one undoubted star that started her distinguished career as a YMCA driver and general help in February 1916. This was Betty Stevenson, who was born in Clifton, York, in 1896. At 14 she was sent away to boarding school in Surrey and from there to Brussels. Her father, Arthur, was a solicitor and for family reasons his family was moved to South Shields, but just before the war they moved to Harrogate, where Arthur switched work to try his hand at estate agency. He presumably did well, because his home was to be Grey Gables in Cavendish Place, a notably impressive Arts and Crafts dwelling in design.

The family supported the work of the YMCA, and this organization, by the time of war, had four bases in Yorkshire with sixty-eight workers. The working of the association was rather similar in spirit to the London settlements for the poor: that is, students participated, and it fulfilled that great ideal of service to others which was inspiring many in the middle classes of the generation born in the 1880s and 1890s. When the war demanded much more of them in the military camps, fund-raising accelerated rapidly.

After all, this is a British affair we are describing, and that being so, the cheeriness went as far as amateur dramatics wherever possible, as shown in this letter from Frank Isherwood:

> We went yesterday to see the Fourth Division Follies, they are a party of pierrots got up by the motor ambulance people. The first part of the performance, consisting of songs in the 'folly' manner... In the interval, one of them came in front of the curtain and told stories. One of them was about the Bishop whose wife wrote a book and also had a child and when a gushing lady complimented him about the child he thought she meant the book and said, 'Wasn't it clever of her – she did it all by herself, she got no help from me and certainly no help from the Archdeacon!'

Clearly, the whole enterprise of voluntary work, not only to treat the troops but also to cheer them, was one of the great success stories of the war (note the reference above: 'got up by the ambulance people').

A card celebrating someone's war effort. (Author's own)

Regarding the YMCA and their key role in this widespread support, they just grew, like Topsy: in 1918 there were fifty-five YMCA huts in Yorkshire. Betty's biographer explains how the organization worked as the war developed:

The YMCA followed troops to the front line and to the sites of conflict scattered across the globe – for this was truly a world

war. As the wounded returned so the YMCA found itself
working alongside the Royal Army Medical Corps in hospitals
and convalescent homes, and in helping relatives to visit their
sons. It also began to provide for the thousands of munitions
workers housed in camps scattered around the country. By 1917
the YMCAs were responsible for 150 munitions workers'
canteens serving c. 200,000 workers daily...

Betty Stevenson was an ideal candidate for a worker within such an
operation. She was energetic, resourceful and courageous. When her
aunt went out to the front in early 1916, Betty wanted to follow and so
she did. The work was unpaid and YMCA workers were volunteers in
every sense; they were alongside the Voluntary Aid Detachment nurses,
essential factors in the support network behind the fighting men. For
Betty, this meant that she would need to buy a car and at a price of
£150 – money raised in Harrogate – she bought a Ford. Her mother
Catherine joined in as well and took a shift when her daughter was
back home. From their records of experience, we can gather a great
deal about their work. In many ways, the demands made on them were
similar to those on the later WVS (Women's Voluntary Service) when
women served abroad, often at the front line or close behind. One
serviceman summed up their role as 'Mother, sister and girlfriend all
in one girl!' We sense that Betty filled exactly those roles in France,
although essentially she was a driver, for pretty much everyone.
  Catherine's description of their workplace speaks volumes about
the conditions and the essential reason for the YMCA being over there:

> It stood for home, and the decencies and amenities of home, and
> we knew it, and it helped us keep going. I know it can be said of
> countless YMCA huts all past these four and a half years, that
> they were little lifeboats in a vast sea of warfare...

Betty became a driver. The essential role is defined by K.V. Yapp:

> When a man was so dangerously wounded that his life was
> despaired of, a message went through to War Office to his wife
> or mother indicating the fact and promising a permit to enable
> them to visit the hospital where the man was lying. The War

Betty Stevenson. (Harrogate Pump Room Museum)

Office form stated that on reaching France the YMCA would look after them. Our motor cars met every boat at Boulogne and Le Havre... Sometimes a long motor run could be accomplished in a few hours, whereas on French railways under war conditions it might have taken days for them to reach their destination...

Betty was based at Étaples, where Vera Brittain more famously worked as a VAD nurse. As with Vera, Betty too was a writer. She wrote letters home and they are very informative about conditions. For example, the following gives a strong impression of her experience:

There was an air fight here yesterday, and a Taube brought down. A piece of our own Archie shell fell outside the YMCA hut, an enormous piece. Could you send me a pair of thick rubber gloves, size 7, ladies. My hands are getting into the most fearful state with messing with the car.

Betty lost her life in France in an air-raid. The *Harrogate Herald* carried this account of her death:

She had been busy all day, in the afternoon at the... and later with the refugees at the station. Owing to a car breaking down a group of workers were later than usual in starting off for... where we have been sending our ladies recently to sleep, for greater safety. A very early raid sent us all to the cellars and after it was over we put the party of two ladies in two cars to send them out of the danger zone, in case the planes returned. We were held up half way, and a second raid came over, forcing us to take shelter under the banks by the side of the road. Everything went well until an enemy plane, just as the raid was finishing, dropped several bombs in open country near us, probably in order to get rid of them before returning. One bomb killed Betty instantly and wounded two other workers, who are in hospital. I was by her side within a minute of the bomb falling, but nothing could be done. She could not have felt it, as she was shot through the left temple. She was taken to hospital at once...

This raid at Étaples was incredibly destructive and frightening. In Nurse de Trafford's diary, she records the details she received of it in her hospital in Lancashire: 'The raid took place on Whit Sunday. On the following Friday, Étaples was bombed again... The St John's Brigade Hospital (which was untouched during the Whit Sunday raid) was terribly wrecked – 13 wards destroyed...'

In January the Military Service Act was passed, and that meant conscription. At that point in the war, 2.6 million men had volunteered for service and, as the war went on, another 2.3 million were to be conscripted. From 1916, service brigades were raised but the Pals battalions were not continued. The situation was that in January of this year conscription of single men was introduced; then, in May, this was extended to all men between the ages of 18 and 41. If they were married or widowed with children or in reserved occupations (e.g. agricultural workers), they were not liable for conscription.

Regarding conscientious objectors and their fate, the tribunal system was created. This meant that a man refusing to enlist had to face a panel of various dignitaries, one of which was a military representative, and plead for exemption from military service. Those who would not even accept non-combatant roles were called 'absolutists' and their destination was prison, with a ridiculous round of court martials and

A contemporary poster showing the almost general attitude to conscientious objectors. (Great War Posters)

prison stretches. In this phase of recruitment, the Ripon camps played a part along with Wakefield prison and Richmond Castle. We have already glanced at one example: that of Ernest England, who was at Ripon Camp. Other such biographies are more obscure.

Obviously, however, various pacifists such as Quakers and those with social or other intellectual bases for their beliefs had a tough time ahead of them after 1916. Ripon played a minor role in this episode of the war, as after 1916 there were some objectors who spent time there but mostly in transit. However, a little further north at Richmond Castle a large number of the more extreme objectors were imprisoned.

The previous year, under the Derby Scheme, men had 'attested', meaning that they had signed a form agreeing to sign up when conscription came along. The reserve battalions were formed and the complement of men in these was 208,500. For men around Harrogate and Ripon, there were local reserve battalions labelled 9th East Yorkshire, 13th West Yorkshire and 11th King's Own Yorkshire Light Infantry, along with the 21st Reserve Brigade which comprised four battalions.

Now the time had come not only for enlistment of the attested men but also for the conscientious objectors to be made public and to face tribunals to decide their fate: whether they would be forcibly dealt with by the army, imprisoned or put to work in non-combatant roles. The difficulties faced by local people in the midst of this may be seen in the case of this tribunal report involving a farmer, for example:

> At the West Riding appeal tribunal at Leeds on Thursday, a Kippax farmer sought exemption for his son, aged 31 and single, who was described as a farm foreman. The appellant declared that the substitute sent to him was no good, and that if his son was taken he would sell up the business.
> Major Dent: Do you realize your duty to your country?
> Farmer: Yes.
> Major Dent: Well, don't talk about selling up. No man has the right to say that in these times.
> The tribunal decided that the case should remain one for substitution.

The papers, as well as the cafes and clubs, were full of philosophical reflections and strong opinions on the nature of conscientious objection. In the *Herald*, one man, William Dewhirst, used a sporting analogy to explain what was a common view:

> Sir, When I was a boy I did not play football: the rough and the tumble and the show toe, and the shinning of those days did not appeal to me. The bed rock bottom truth was that I was a bit afraid. I did not say that. I simply told my friends that I did not care for the game. I read today that there are conscientious objectors. I suppose that I was one. But I have often assisted a schoolfellow from the football field to his home; I never thought of leaving him to get there the best that he could for the fear that he might recover from his injury and play again. There are many genuine objectors to war. There are more than a few genuine humbugs. I was a coward as regards football, but I had a spark of humanity in me to which I am ever thankful.

The debate went on into 1917, testing the logic as well as the emotional commitment to the war, increasingly so as time went on and losses mounted in the numbers of the dead.

In early June that year, a young man called Barbellion wrote this entry in his diary:

> This morning in bed I heard a man with a milk cart say in the road to a villager at about 6.30 a.m. 'battle... and we lost six cruisers.' This was the first I knew of the Battle of Jutland. At 8 a.m. I read in the *Daily News* that the British Navy had been defeated, and thought it was the end of all things. The news took away our appetites. At the railway station the *Morning Post* was more cheerful, even reassuring, and now at 6.30 p.m. the battle has turned into a merely regrettable indecisive action. We breathe once more.

As this hints, Jutland was big news. The German fleet had been penned in, tight, in the Baltic ports by the British navy for some time. Then, at the end of May, the Germans turned and attacked the British who were commanded by Sir John Jellicoe. It was not exactly a significant result for Britain. One summary of the British Grand Fleet has this criticism:

'The Grand Fleet's rangefinders were deficient, its target-plotting machinery prone to error, and its gunnery computers, staff work and armoured protection defective.'

In Harrogate the papers featured the loss of Knaresborough man Daniel Dempsey of Scriven, who was lost on HMS *Tipperary* which was sunk in the battle. In the end he had to be supposed drowned because, as the paper reported:

> A week after the news of the battle was published, Mr and Mrs Dempsey received an Admiralty communication to the effect that their son was supposed to have been drowned. Later, however, the Germans reported that they had saved seven members of the crew of the destroyer... and Mr and Mrs Dempsey did not give up hope. Nothing further has been heard, and it is supposed that Seaman Dempsey went down with his ship.

Daniel was just 19 and a former pupil at Priory Street School, York. He had been working in a York printer's office before enlisting.

The camps were still busy in 1916, of course, as they were always destined to be. Things seemed to be improving in terms of troops and town relations, as a film made for the Ripon Palladium Cinema shows. It was shown to the locals in May that year and it shows Ripon folk joining in with their military guests in a sports day; the film shows some smiling, relaxed men from Scottish regiments who were enjoying such entertainments as races, athletics and bayonet-charging contests, all to the accompaniment of a bagpiper.

Not everyone enjoyed camp life, however. Ripon over the war years saw many a famous literary man stationed there while in khaki, and in the autumn of this year the Bradford writer J.B. Priestley was there as a lance corporal in the Duke of Wellington's regiment. He was not keen on the place, as shown by his words of 1933 when he penned *English Journey*. He recalled his time in Ripon in a miserable tone:

> I found myself in what was called, by some ironic jester at the War Office, a 'convalescent camp'. Actually it was not a camp fit for troops bursting with health; and for genuine convalescents it was a nightmare of mud, bad food and petty tyrannies. I do not know what beribboned ass was responsible for the miseries

of that camp – but even after all these years I am not ready to forgive either him or his ghost.

Priestley said that he was 'herded into the camp like a diseased sheep.' Criticism and complaint are built into the psyche of soldiers, of course, and the stereotype of the 'old sweat', as in Bruce Bairnsfather's cartoons, is never far from Priestley's account of his war. He wrote in one of his autobiographical volumes: 'In my company there were a few suburban junior clerks and the like... and the closer of these, whose names I still remember, were all killed... Perhaps it was the Irish in them that lifted their grumbling, which never stopped, to an Elizabethan height.' However, he does, in the same memoir, say rather more about his camp life:

> Our average programme was ten hours a day, and nobody grumbled more than the old regulars... We began without any equipment at all. There was not enough khaki cloth for regulation uniforms... It was only in musketry that we were far behind the Regular Army, simply because we had to wait for months for the rifles we would eventually use.

Regarding Ripon, he adds something else to the account given in *English Journey*:

> I was dispatched for further treatment to a convalescent camp at Ripon. There I was miserable, like everybody else I knew. It was a bad camp, so bad, that not long afterwards, I believe, the men mutinied. There was too much mud, too many restrictions, too many P.T. instructors swelling their chests, which had never known a front line parapet.... To hell with them and their jump to it!

Fortunately for Priestley, he was removed to Alnwick camp after the Ripon experience and things improved for him. As to the mutiny, there appears to be no evidence of that.

Over in France, by early summer matters intensified and also switched to a much more large-scale affair. As John Buchan, writing just after the war, says:

By June, 1916 the term New Armies was a misnomer. The whole British force, in one sense, was new. The famous old regiments of the line had been completely renewed since Mons and their drafts drawn from the same source as the men of the new battalions... If the Old Army bore the brunt of the First Battle of Ypres, the Territorials were no less heroic in the Second Battle of Ypres, and the new army had to its credit the four-mile charge at Loos.

At the beginning of July, the Battle of the Somme began. The British had as their objective the defeat of the Germans in their first position. From north to south, this went from Gommecourt, north-west of Bapaume, to Soycourt, after running close by Albert. The names along that route are now, in modern parlance, iconic. Names where significant actions occurred are endlessly described and discussed, and the roll of honour relating the men's heroism is never read with a sense of duty but rather with a deep sense of respect and admiration. Some of those distinguished actions in the theatre of war were carried out by Harrogate and Ripon men and during the course of events between July and November, two more men from the Harrogate area were to win the Victoria Cross, following that award to Charles Hull in 1915.

The first of these men, Second Lieutenant Donald Bell, won his VC for his endeavours on 5 July when he carried out a bold and effective bombing of a machine-gun position. This was part of the first phase of the Battle of the Somme. On the first day of the battle, 19,240 British soldiers lost their lives and 5,000 tons of ammunition was aimed at the German positions on each day. Infantry charged trench positions and the slaughter was great. In just one day, 248 men of the Leeds Pals Battalion were killed.

In one of these early actions, Lieutenant Bell was distinguished. He was born in 1890

Donald Bell, footballer and war hero. (Harrogate Pump Room Museum) and attended St Peter's Church of England Primary School and Harrogate Grammar School, and then went on to London to study at Westminster College. From an early age he showed high ability in sports and games and became a professional footballer, playing with several teams but being mostly remembered for his time at Bradford Park Avenue FC. After playing football as an amateur, he came back to Harrogate and became a teacher at Starbeck Council School, signing on for Bradford in 1912.

Donald was the first professional footballer to enlist in the army in 1914, being commissioned into the Green Howards, the 9th Battalion of the Princess of Wales's Own Yorkshire Regiment. Before the events leading to the VC, correspondence in the Breare columns of the *Herald* progressed apace. In June, his brother Billy Bell wrote home to Breare: 'Last night my brother Don Bell called to see me on his way home on leave, and we spent about two hours together. I wished I was coming too, for Harrogate must be looking well by now, but I must wait two or three months before my turn comes.' He also mentions other Harrogate men he had met at the front.

The modern reader, following Breare's column, can track Bell's progress up to 5 July when he won his VC. He was the son of Mr and Mrs Smith Bell of East Parade in Harrogate and only five weeks before he was killed – while home on leave after seeing his brother – he married Miss R.M. Bonson at Kirkby Stephen.

There are few more touching pieces of writing in all the reports relating to Harrogate men in that war than Breare's account of the VC and then of the death of Bell. He begins with an account of the action:

Second Lieutenant Don Bell was in charge of the bombing section. The boys who were to make the rush went on. Soon a German gun was discovered somewhere on their flank enfilading their ranks and doing much damage. Don Bell took some bombers in the direction of this gun. They crawled on their hands and knees ever so far until within about twenty yards of the offending gun. Bell threw one bomb, and in that first shot blew the gun to smithereens. The party then stormed the German trench and sent fifty Germans below. Next day the General Officer Commanding came to the regiment and thanked them for the success of that great movement, for it had been entirely successful...

Bell wrote home and included an account of what he had done. Characteristically, it downplayed his own part and was written with a tone of notable modesty, but all that was too much for Breare, who wanted always to give credit where it was due. The latter wrote:

> He tells the outline of the tale, but his narrative was too fettered with modesty... with him was a nice lad of 19, and Bell declares that this lad did all the work... We won't allow anybody to run our boys down... A fluke indeed! We have only to inquire what a fluke is to know how far Don is wrong in his estimate... A fluke is an accomplishment by an unskilled person... in other words, an occurrence due to accident rather than skill. Now too many of us know Don Bell as one of our finest athletes... We are quite ready to give the nice little chap of 19 every credit for his brave and successful assistance. But Harrogate is jealous of its reputation and its honours...

Bell was one of a number of men who distinguished themselves at the Somme for the Green Howards. Geoffrey and John Powell, in their history of the regiment, explain: '... as Lieutenant-Colonel Fife remarked, most of the sixteen individuals he had recommended on one occasion for gallantry awards would, in the old days, have qualified for a Victoria Cross.'

The shock five days later was horrendous. Poor Breare had to report Bell's death, in an operation similar to the one of the 5th: 'Don Bell has fallen. A brief telegram tells us so. There is just a gleam of sunshine to lighten our despair. In his last letter he charged his loved ones to be of good heart and fear not. His very last words were, "I am in God's hands."' This was all in a context in which around 600,000 casualties had been entered in the statistics in less than five months. In the first action of the Somme, the Green Howards' 2nd Battalion alone had lost 200 men.

The effects of Bell's death were profoundly moving. There was even a poem to him in the pages of the *Herald*, which had the lines: 'His was the death he would have wished to die, an Englishman – a gentleman – a man.'

The full story of his death soon appeared in the press. His CO, Lieutenant Colonel Holmes, wrote a clear account:

An image from the first day of the Battle of the Somme. (John Buchan, The Battle of the Somme)

On the 10th this battalion, with another of the Yorkshire Regiment, attacked and captured a very important village. The Germans again did not stand, and large numbers of prisoners were taken and eight machine guns etc. Unfortunately our numbers who attacked the village were few, and the Germans endeavoured to come back and work behind us. Your son headed a bombing party which drove off the German attack, and once again saved the situation. Unfortunately he was himself shot...

The scrap at Contalmaison had been hard indeed. In one early account of the action at La Boisselle, Ovillers and Contalmaison, the point is made: 'But our success at Contalmaison was beyond our strength to maintain, and in the afternoon a counter-attack forced us back into the village.' Contalmaison was only 3 miles north of Mametz Wood, where there had been immense loss of life a little earlier, notably among the Welsh regiments.

In Breare's columns in the *Herald* the tributes flowed, many from other Tommies who knew Don Bell. The place of his death was Contalmaison, a few miles north-east of Albert, and the location of his action was marked and remembered, with his name attached, as Bell's Redoubt. One old friend, Private P.J. Cullingworth, wrote: 'He used to be a very intimate friend of mine when he was at Starbeck School. I was living in hopes of meeting him out here... but Fate has decreed otherwise... Harrogate has lost one of its best athletes...'

Then, on 13 September, the announcement came and the *Herald* reported: 'Harrogate people deeply regret that Second Lieutenant Donald S. Bell does not live to wear the Victoria Cross, which his gallant conduct secured him a few days before his lamented death.' The award goes with the following citation:

> For most conspicuous bravery. During an attack a very heavy enfilade fire was opened on the attacking Company by a hostile machine-gun. Second Lieutenant Bell immediately and on his own crept up a communication trench and then, followed by Corporal Colwill and Private Batey, rushed across the open under heavy fire, and attacked the machine-gun, shooting the firer with his revolver and destroying the gun and personnel with bombs.

In 1917 there was a ceremony at Starbeck Council School as a tablet to Bell's memory was unveiled. Local dignitaries attended, and the mayor made a point of referring to the 'great sacrifice made in defence of King and country. Bell's working life had started at that school, as he was a student-teacher from 1st August, 1908 to 31 July, 1909 and it was during this time that he showed the promise of becoming an extremely successful teacher.'

Of course, there were regular messages about deaths and severe woundings, most being nowhere near as detailed accounts as those of Bell. On 23 August, for instance, we have a footnote to the horror and suffering, which was becoming increasingly common, when the *Herald* reported: 'Private R. Winn, Northumberland Fusiliers, had his right arm blown off in the big advance of July 1st. He formerly worked at Mr Charlton's farm, Docken Bush, near Ripley.' In a letter home, the famed Tommy spirit comes through in abundance: 'I am going on fine.

I can get about a bit now my arm is almost healed up. It is off just below the elbow, but never mind, it might have been a lot worse.'

There is no shortage of information now about individual soldiers at the Somme, thanks to the labours of family historians. A typical example of this is the tale of two Ripon brothers, whose story was told to the press by Pete Colman in 2014. The first, Stanley Cooper-Tempest, was in the West Yorkshire Regiment and at the Somme he had a serious injury to his shoulder, then being stretchered off, and as he was on the move he recalled seeing a Ripon man he knew with part of his leg blown off; the latter was a man who amazingly survived.

Stan's handed-down story has elements of really close-up social history, such as the account of him being ordered to go to the shed and take his combat clothes off because they were alive with vermin such as lice.

In France Stan saw his brother, Gordon, while on the march and he only knew because someone shouted: 'Hey Temp... just seen your lad down the road!' Gordon's enlistment was one of those typical tales we read of the rules being slightly bent to accommodate the enthusiastic young: he was too young, but was told to take a walk and then come back as by that time he would be old enough to join. Gordon was to become a prisoner of war and he had a harrowing tale to tell, suffering near-starvation.

In October came another VC from the area. Again, it was awarded to a Green Howards' man. In the last days of September and early October, near Thiepval, Captain Archie White distinguished himself by continually risking his life. He had become a staff officer on 30 June and was later to be made a brigade major.

The following citation for his VC describes the action leading to the award:

For most conspicuous bravery at Stuff Redoubt on 27 September and 1 October 1916. Captain White was in command of the troops that held the southern and western faces of a redoubt for four days and nights. By his indomitable spirit, great personal courage and skilful dispositions, he held his position under fire of all kinds and against several counter-attacks. Although short of supplies and ammunition his determination never wavered. When the enemy attacked in greatly superior numbers he led a counter-attack which finally cleared the enemy from the southern and westward faces. He risked his life continually and was the life and soul of defence.

This was within an overall context in which Germany wanted to hold firm and allow the Allies to come at them. As John Buchan put it:

> The Allied aim must be clearly understood. It was not to recover so many square miles of France; it was not to take Bapaume or Peronne... it was not even in the strictest sense to carry this or that position... That purpose was simply to exercise a steady and continued pressure on a certain section of the enemy's front.

Archie White certainly played his part in that; it was a war of attrition and the best ploy was to hold firm and cause trouble. He was born in 1891 at Boroughbridge and studied at Harrogate Grammar School, then reading English at King's College, London. Following that he began a career in teaching before the war came along. Joining the Green Howards, he was involved in the Gallipoli campaign where his brother John was killed.

White survived the war and relinquished his commission in November 1920. He then joined the Army Education Corps and worked in that capacity during the Second World War. He had also won the Military Cross, so as an instructor at Sandhurst he had an impressive array of letters after his name: Major A.C.T. White VC, MC and also BA. He died on 20 May 1971 at his home in Camberley, Surrey.

By 1916 the war was dominating everything. The country knew that it was in the midst of a huge, all-consuming trajectory of international conflict that was drawing in the lands of the Empire, and that despite censorship the publishing industry was churning out memoirs and information. In this year, for instance, one publisher produced a series headed 'Soldiers' Tales of the Great War' and their titles included *With My Regiment* by 'Platoon Commander' and *Uncensored Letters from the Dardanelles*, the notes of a French army doctor. People of all kinds had their stories to tell, from Gomez Carillo's *Among the Ruins* to *The Drama of 365 Days* by Hall Caine.

Some books stood out as exceptional, providing graphic insights into specific tasks being done heroically behind the lines, coping with the dead, the dying and the wounded. The Quakers and other categories of non-combatant pacifists worked in ambulance units and even war correspondents did such work when needed, as was the case with Philip Gibbs, whose 1916 book, *The Soul of War*, is arguably worthy of the word 'classic'. His account of medical stretcher-work is extremely powerful, and if we need to understand what the non-combatants were doing by 1916 when the Somme had made it plain that the death toll was dauntingly high, then Gibbs is the man to read:

> I helped to carry out the body, as everyone helped to do any small work if he had his hands free at the moment. It was the saving of one's sanity and self-respect... Not all the skill of the surgeons could patch up some of those bodies, torn open with ghastly wounds from German shells. The smell of wet and muddy clothes, coagulated blood and gangrened limbs, of iodine and chloroform, sickness and sweat of agony, made a stench which struck one's senses with a foul blow. I used to try and close my nostrils to it, holding my breath lest I should vomit...

At the heart of the overarching tale that came from France, the Battle of the Somme stands supreme. The battle represents the fearful arithmetic of mass death and the accounts of the months over which it extended, particularly July and August, form a compelling literature of their own. One manuscript diary with 'Commencement of the Battle of the Somme July 1st' written along the side of a page, is in large letters, and the soldier – an artilleryman – has written an entry for that momentous date that immediately gives an insight into the event:

> Today the big attack on the Germans commenced. Reveille was at 4 a.m. At 8 a.m. the battery turned out in full marching order and paraded on the gun park, hooked into the limbers ready to move off if the infantry advance was sufficiently successful to require the guns moving forward. Everyone was keenly excited and expectant, for now 'open warfare' was anticipated and the beginning of the end. However, after standing ready all the morning the parade was dismissed...

That one brief diary entry has all the ingredients of that great occasion and of the mindset of that point in the war: a matter-of-fact precision; a touch of humour; and, most of all, a reflection of what the general attitudes were and how wrong they turned out to be. Most poignant of all is the phrase 'open warfare', which carries with it a terrible irony.

The Somme was a landmark in a number of ways. As Philip Warner pointed out, it '... marked the midway part of the war but at the time it seemed the culmination of everyone's efforts and therefore a time to arrange a peace.' There would be talk of such a thing, even in the midst of such a deadlock. Yet it also established a pattern and a scenario: the theatre of war in this particular conflict had been transformed from a brief affair into an epic narrative. The battle was always going to be an affair of mythic proportions and the mass deaths, along with the basic failure of the allied bombardment before the infantry advanced, will always attract the analyses of the military historians. However, this will never move from centre-stage the almost endless family stories – including those still being discovered – of individual heroism and sacrifice.

As mentioned in the previous chapter, Harrogate, along with the rest of Yorkshire, felt the effects of the Barnbow munitions factory disaster in 1916: an explosion at its 200-acre site in Crossgates, north of Leeds. Barnbow employed 16,000 women and another 1,000 men. On 5 December, as some women were putting fuses to shells (which were packed with explosive), a huge explosion shook the whole place. There were thirty-five deaths and a large number of injuries. However, the workers were paid £12 a week and the shells were urgently needed, so in spite of this horrific accident, the management had to move quickly and have the place up and running again within a very short time.

The work was tough, starting at six in the morning, and production never stopped, not even for public holidays. One report has noted: 'The girls would inscribe cheeky messages on shells for the amusement of soldiers... Working with TNT induced jaundice (earning them the nickname of "canary girls") and other serious illnesses, including rotting teeth.'

Thanks to determined research by Ann Batchelor and others, we now know a lot more about the women who died at Barnbow. As she has pointed out, for wartime purposes of morale and reportage, publicity at the time was greatly reduced. The factory was vast, having been extended to 400 acres, and a special railway line was used to move the larger shells; clearly this was dangerous work as it involved working with fuses, and it appears that this explosion was caused by a poorly-fixed fuse that had a spark alight on it.

There is now a list of those who died. There were fifty-seven deaths in all, and these included James Thompson of Harrogate who clung on to life until 31 May and two Harrogate women, Ada Glassby and Emily Sedgewick.

There were also heroic tales, notably that of William Parkin who went into the place a dozen times to try to rescue people. Ann Batchelor has steadily gathered information, as has Carol Smithies who, for instance, interviewed Sally Howe some years ago and Sally was then a centenarian who had worked at the factory as a teenager.

Even more than a year after the Barnbow explosion, there was still discussion of how much and for what reasons the munitions workers' demanding and dangerous conditions could be alleviated. The *Yorkshire Post* of 7 August 1916 reported on a 'relay system': 'According to prominent labour leaders, who have been consulted, the interim report declares in favour of a brief period of rest for all munitions workers in certain conditions regarding length of service and good time-keeping.' One would have thought that with the privations and risks involved in the work and the frequency of life-threatening accidents, there would have been more urgent reform.

This was just one part of the huge, urgent national effort to produce munitions to feed the war. Gerard de Groot has explained the source of this issue: 'Once stalemate descended upon the western front, however, heavy guns became transcendent. Only high-calibre, high explosive shells were even remotely effective against a heavily entrenched enemy.'

Munitions production was very dangerous work. There were toxic fumes to contend with and at any moment a shell might explode. Yet the job had to be done and it provided employment for almost 1 million women. There was, of course, the sorority of the job. One worker recalled: 'It was just magic, we worked and we stood and we sat and we sang. If anyone had come into the factory they never would have believed what had gone on.'

CHAPTER 4

1917
Casualties, Heroes and Survival

This year was to bring an intensification of the U-boat menace in the Channel and the North Sea and the subsequent responses and tactics of the British navy, including the arrival of the Q-ships, which were battleships in disguise, posing as simple merchant vessels. It was also the year of Operation ALBERICH, which was the German consolidation of defences along the Hindenburg Line. Regarding the principal battles, these were, in the first phase of the year, at Arras, and outstandingly at Hill 145, in which Vimy Ridge figured, and the distinguished combat of the Canadian forces. There were huge casualties: around 10,000 from the Canadian ranks. Then there was the war in the air, which was also extended and intensified. There was a call for trainee pilots and recruits came from the army as well as from home.

Massive confrontations followed in terrifying sequence throughout the year: Messines in June; the Third Battle of Ypres from July to November; Cambrai at the end of the year and, with that, the escalation of the use of tanks in the war. The sources across the board, from theatre of war to home front, indicate a sustained lull in morale and a sense of futility and insensate resignation to the privations and sufferings that were being experienced everywhere.

Wars tend to have a trajectory that is defined by increasing chaos and confusion, and a world war throws people around at will as pragmatic decisions have to be made and sheer exigency applies pressure to all. The most unexpected encounters tend to happen and surprising paths sometimes cross as fate directs everyone in accordance with necessity. Such was the case in Harrogate in 1917, when a subsequently very famous writer stayed in the town. The man in question was J.R.R. Tolkien, author of the cult classic *The Lord of the Rings*. Tolkien, now with the 11th Lancashire Fusiliers and on his way to coastal guard duty out at Roos in the East Riding, was suffering from trench fever and his recovery was very slow. He was officially in Furness Auxiliary Hospital but was given three weeks' leave and stayed at 95 Valley Drive, not far from the Baths, and in the Montpellier Quarter today.

Valley Drive, where J.R.R. Tolkien stayed in 1917. (Author's own)

He met his friend, Christopher Wiseman, in the town on 18 April. According to John Garth, Tolkien's most recent biographer, Wiseman came to Harrogate and announced that he was going to 'burst into... literary solitudes… so here's to the Council of Harrogate!' In other words, for Tolkien, his stay in the town was happy: it lived up to its reputation as a wholesome, curative location with rather more than merely material comforts; it helped with the regeneration of creative energy too.

On the world stage, however, the opening of 1917 meant that the U-boat threat was intensifying and in April and May, the Battle of Arras was to take place. Over 2,000 allied ships would be lost throughout the year.

More homely and chatty was one of Breare's topics early in the year. One has the sense sometimes when reading Breare's slangy and jocular comments and responses to servicemen's letters that war had become a way of life, something as familiar as fish and chips. In March this year his thoughts on Wireless Officer Cecil Potts have that characteristic. Nevertheless, it is a reflection on the horrors of the submarine war that was in progress. Breare begins: 'This morning a very smart young fellow called in. He was dressed in a sort of naval uniform, which I had not noticed before. On his cap was the letter 'M' and on his shoulders a gold waved line.' He turned out to be Wireless Operator C. Potts, son of Mr and Mrs Potts of Mayfield Grove.

Potts had been in London, training as a Marconi operator. A month later, Breare had a letter from Potts, who had written to describe his life as a tar. He was grounded for training and wrote: 'I call it jolly hard lines because I wanted to be on the briny chasing old Fritz and his submarines.' Potts, Breare reports, then chats about meeting an old friend from Harrogate, and so we have a chirpy, morale-boosting account of comradeship and thoughts of home: 'We had a good old chat about "the best place in the world" (you know, Harrogate). Before he enlisted he was with Snow and Ashworth's, the jewellers on Cambridge Crescent.'

The Potts story then opens out into a sad template for so many young lives in that war because Breare, writing in November, reports that he had not seen Potts since Easter. Then, in December, we have this about Potts: 'I do not think that I have told you that he is at home now suffering from shell shock. After he called to see me, he went to sea again, was torpedoed and lost all his belongings.' In January 1918, Potts went off to sea again. Breare adds 'he anticipates that there will be no torpedoing this time.'

The whole story serves several purposes, mainly that of being cheery, downplaying situations of extreme fear and horror, with Potts singled out as a matey rating from the greatest navy in the world, as all Breare's readers would have been thinking. Yet behind this lies the greater, overarching story of the German U-boat attacks. In August 1914, at the very beginning of the war, there had been casualties at sea as HMS *Amphion* was sunk in the North Sea. Then at the Battle of Jutland from 31 May to 1 June 1916, Britain lost fourteen ships and there were over 6,000 fatalities. The sinking of the *Lusitania* the year before had already told civilians just how dangerous sea voyages were likely to be.

Yet, of course, Breare could not avoid having to retail the tragedies as well. In February he learned of the loss of the son of Councillor Knowles. Breare wrote of this, again humanizing and localizing every feature of the material:

> I have just learnt with great sorrow that Harry has been killed. He was in a dugout having his tea when a shell struck it, killing him and two other boys. A fourth soldier had gone out on duty and asked his comrades to have his tea ready. When the fourth returned they were digging the three out of the wrecked dugout. It is quite possible they may be Harrogate boys. The loss of anyone's boys touches us, yet it is only natural that our main anxiety is for our own.

Again, Breare brings his readers imaginatively almost into the homes of his subjects: 'The late Councillor Knowles's sister died some years before he passed away, so there is now no-one left of the little household save a cousin, Miss Batters...'

The stories of Harrogate and Ripon men involved in action at sea are, naturally, comparatively few. However, another man to see something of Jutland was Able Seaman Ingleson, who was involved in a most dramatic confrontation. He joined the navy at just 15, served on the destroyer *St Vincent* and then transferred to HMS *Broke*, another destroyer. On the new vessel, he was distinguished in a very exceptional and impressive way, as the *Herald* reported, describing what happened when two enemy destroyers opened fire on the *Broke*:

> The foremost gun crews were reduced from 18 men to six. Midshipman Donald Gyles, RNR, in charge of the forecastle, though wounded in the eye, kept all foremost guns in action, himself assisting the depleted guns to reload. While he was thus employed a number of frenzied Germans swarmed up over the *Broke*'s forecastle guns, swept aft in a shouting mob. The midshipman, amid the dead and wounded... met the rush single-handed with an automatic revolver. He was grappled by a German... the German was promptly bayoneted by Able Seaman Ingleson. The remainder of the invaders, with the exception of two who lay down and feigned death, were driven over the side...

Breare was in triumphant print at this, of course. He wrote that '...thanks to the bravery of our Harrogate lads, the town is frequently reaping high, reflected honours.' He also pointed out that the famous Captain Evans of Scott's ill-fated 'Polar Party' had at one time commanded the *Broke*.

This was actually a phase in what is now known as the Battle of Dover Strait, which took place on 20/21 April 1917; technically the second scrap of that name as there was another in the previous year, but the 1917 action is generally regarded as the major battle at that location. The scene described by Breare, featuring the hand-to-hand fighting, captured the imagination of the press and Ingleson featured in a front-page illustration in the hugely popular series *The War Illustrated*.

Nevertheless, the encounter of the *Swift* and the *Broke* with the German ships was fierce and violent, so much so that the *Broke* was very seriously damaged and had to be towed back to port.

However, no chatty newspaper features could stave off the pain of the bad news of men missing or dead. Arguably, an instance of this at this time, relating to the confrontation at Beaumont Hamel, illustrates the nature of the sad news in question and the soldier concerned was Sergeant Oliver Gaundry. The context is the battle in the Ancre Valley and the fight in which Gaundry was involved was a to-and-fro trench struggle at Ten Tree Alley. On 10 February the British of 32nd Division

12th May. 1917.   No. 143. Vol. 6.

THE WAR
Illustrated

A PICTURE-RECORD of Events by Land, Sea and Air.   Edited by J. A. HAMMERTON

HEROIC MIDDY OF H.M.S. BROKE.— Fine incident of the recent fight when H.M.S. Broke and Swift defeated six enemy destroyers and sank two of them. Midshipman Donald A. Gyles, R.N.R., single-handed met an enemy boarding-party, one of whom, grappling, sought to wrest his revolver from him. Able-Seaman Ingleson came to the officer's support and promptly bayoneted the German.

Able Seaman Ingleson: an image of the young hero. (The War Illustrated)

took the trench, east of Beaumont. It was very cold and the whole enterprise was severely demanding on the men. The Germans staged a counter-attack on the 11th and it seems that Gaundry was wounded in that fight. In fact, there were 232 British casualties in that stage of the battle. He survived that and was wounded again later, in May.

Sergeant Gaundry was from Galphay, Ripon, and had joined the West Yorkshire Regiment in late 1914. After training in Harrogate, he was in France soon after, and in the Roll of Honour we have the following, after stating that he had been wounded and missing since 3 May:

> A letter from his officer states: Your son went into action on the morning of May 3rd, and has not been seen since. We are almost certain he was taken prisoner, as his party was cut off in the rear... I am unable to tell you how much we miss him...

Breare also used some considerable column space to write about Gunner Percy Raworth in 1917. The background to his story is the Battle of Cambrai, in which tanks were prominent, and in fact it was a momentous occasion because it was the first time that tanks had been used as the spearhead. They had been used before but disappointingly, as at Passchendaele and the Somme. However, this time General Haig planned carefully and took advice on the matter. The action was to be an advance to the Hindenburg Line, just a short distance away from the line held by the Allies which, south to north, went from close to Vendhuile up to near Moeuvres. In the central area was Havrincourt Wood. With the big guns kept behind ready for the usual German counter-attack, the advance of the tanks began – 381 of them – followed by infantry and then cavalry.

The unexpected turn of events – and it was in this that Raworth died – was that in the counter-attack, the Germans used planes. On 2 October Breare wrote: 'We have had another severe blow, in the death of Percy Raworth, whom you will remember as of the tanks. He is the only son of my friend Councillor Raworth.' At that point, Breare did not know the circumstances of Raworth's death. Earlier in the year, Raworth had been reported as being at Thiepval with Private Ben Thorpe, who was hit by shrapnel in that fight.

On 10 October, Breare learned of Raworth's death in the aerial

Edna the Tank: one of the tanks that did the tour of the land as part of the Tank Week fund-raising campaign. (Laura Carter)

attack and he printed a letter from Captain Robinson, addressed to Raworth's father, saying: 'Just a line to let you know the sad news. Percy Raworth was killed on Sunday while guarding one of the animals. He volunteered for this guard, and was left by himself. A bomb from an aeroplane fell close to him, which practically killed him outright.'

Finally, it was learned that Raworth had won a medal and that there was much more to it than his simply guarding an animal:

After our tank had stuck he jumped out and assisted in digging it out for fourteen and a half hours under very heavy fire. Your son worked in a most exposed position, thus setting a fine example of pluck and endurance to the remainder of the crew. A comrade says he was struck by an enemy aeroplane bomb and continues, 'He was made as comfortable as it was humanly possible under the circumstances... You have lost a good son and we have lost a popular chum – one who was always cheerful and ready to help others...'

Percy Raworth was awarded the Military Medal.

All this shows, once again, just how much Breare's contribution was valued and how he came to recognize the importance of playing down the dark side and stressing the cheeriness and good spirits. He was always keen to share and disseminate the Tommies' resilient humour and he gave this a Harrogate focus.

At Passchendaele, even the national reporters for the major presses made a special mention of the Yorkshire contribution, as shown by this extract headed 'Where the Advance Sagged: Yorkshiremen's Battle in Marsh and Fog':

> Yesterday I spent a large part of the day with certain Yorkshire troops. The story of their advance is typical of that part of the field where we did not succeed... No man started to attack that morning who was not already weary and soaked, and partly numbed, covered with slime from falling into shell-holes and chilled with standing hip-high in icy water. It was only half-light, and a thick white mist enfolded the battlefield... Floundering, wading, and helping each other along amid bursting shells and a storm of machine-gun bullets, it was more than an hour's hard work for our men to force their way across those four or five hundred yards...

The stories of Harrogate people from the various front-line areas of conflict kept coming in and some had significant achievements. One of the most remarkable was another Royal Red Cross winner from the Salonika campaign, although she had been active in several parts of the map of war. This was Assistant Matron Lily Agnes Ephgrave, who was born in Linthorpe and whose family home was in Harrogate during the war. She trained for her first nursing qualification in Liverpool. At the outbreak of war she volunteered, and worked with the Queen Alexandra Imperial Military Nursing Service after having attested for them in 1906. She was to have an extraordinarily distinguished career.

In Salonika in 1917 she was Mentioned in Despatches while under the command of General Milne 'for her valuable services with the forces in the field.' What she was up against in that context was, in particular, malaria but of course there was large-scale conflict, particularly after the attack at Lake Doiran in which there were 5,000

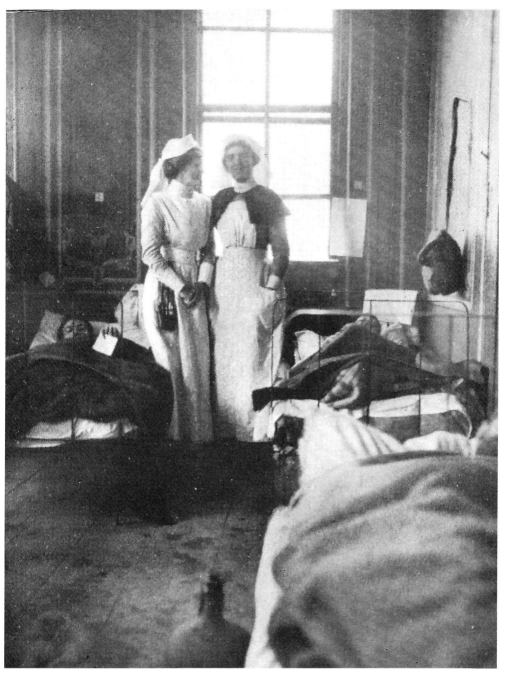

A typical hospital ward during the war. (Mrs Stobart, War and Women*)*

British dead and wounded. She herself contracted influenza in Salonika and managed to survive.

She stayed on after the war, serving in a number of places, and was invalided out from Egypt in 1931. She said that she was completely worn out from hard work, the trials of the climate and the testing nature of her work. Lily Ephgrave's memory is marked by a string of medals, as she had the Royal Red Cross, the medal for Mentioned in Despatches and several others. There were many others like Lily and their names are rarely remembered in any significant way, but she was representative of that quiet, determined dedication to duty that sustained the fighting men through so many hard years.

At home, insights into the problems and issues being encountered in everyday life are easily gleaned from the press. One feature that is often noted is the more frequent criticisms of the War Office and of the difficulties relating to conscription. In the *Primitive Methodist Leader*, for instance, in which paragraphs of news summaries provide a useful chronicle of events, we have the following:

> If we were not living in extraordinary times, it is difficult to see how any government could survive the crumbling indictment which Mr Asquith brought on the War Office for their maladministration of the Review of Exceptions Act, in their calling up of notoriously unfit, and in some instances, of dead men...

Breare, chatting and updating furiously as usual, mentioned several men working at the *Herald* offices and made a point of mentioning a colleague: '*Herald* staff boys and others who know him will be pleased to hear that Gill, one of our staff... has not been given exemption only till January. There is no date to his exemption, so I hope he will not be troubled again.'

There were also shortages, of course, and these were beginning to pinch by this time. Butter was hard to find and Breare was shocked to learn that he had heard of Danish butter being sold at 4s a pound. He opined that 'we shall have to fall back on dripping.' Coal was expensive too: in 1917 the price rose to 32s 6d a ton, and transport equally became more costly. Breare painted a vivid picture of the shortages:

> I suppose the scenes on Saturday night at the shops wherever butter and tea are sold were something extraordinary. Empty shelves proved the shortage, and many people went unsatisfied. The tea difficulty is very acute just now. Customers in most cases obtained ounces instead of pounds... The cheapest tea is now said to be 4s a pound...

The shortages naturally had a profound effect on morale. The eternal inventiveness and guile of business people prevailed, though, as the producers worked hard to change attitudes. As Gerard de Groot wrote in his history of the home front: '"Everyone has less money to spend on food" one advertisement lamented. The wise ones make nourishing Quaker Oats the stand-by.... Your family won't miss expensive bacon and eggs if you serve delicious Quaker Oats.' Bread, the staff of life, was a major issue. Loaves were adapted; that is, made differently with more use of potato flour and grains other than wheat. This did not affect sales, however, as consumption rose during this year. The media got firmly behind all attempts to help the housewife, of course, as in the production of such things as the *Win-the-War Cookery Book* with its fighting words: 'The struggle is not only on land and sea; it is in your larder, your kitchen and your dining-room. Every meal you serve is now literally a battle.'

In one of Breare's comments we have a hint of a tragic story that lies behind his brief comment. He noted that Lady Enid Vane had been selling flags to raise money and that her husband had died of wounds. He was only 35 years old. Lady Enid worked as a volunteer in one of the Harrogate hospitals. In fact, she had married Major Hon. Henry Cecil Vane just after the outbreak of war on 25 August 1914. She was the daughter of Anthony Mildmay Fane, the 13th Earl of Westmoreland. Unusually, her marriage entailed the change of just one letter of her name. Major Vane was injured in October 1917 and died in a hospital in France. Enid eventually married again, in 1922, to Major Herbert Turner.

At the Ripon camps there were continuing problems and issues. In their first phase of development, the main topics of controversy had related to the clash of city and camp, as already mentioned. By 1917, what was foremost was the view that the camps were riddled with disease and were likely to spread the most horrendous illnesses across the county. One man who responded forcefully to this accusation was the Mayor of Ripon, Frederick Hargrave, and he wrote this letter to the *Herald*:

> The Health of Ripon Camp
> Sir,
> As these rumours reflect, not only on the medical staff there, but also upon our city, may I say that I am informed from an official source that since the camp was started in May last year, the actual sickness rate has been under two per cent and the death rate under two per thousand.

However, it is easy to understand the general fears in this regard. After all, the local papers were packed with reports from the hospitals: there was a regular feature in the *Herald* on 'Chats with the Wounded' and this covered the whole assemblage of places from Beaulieu Hospital to St George's Convalescent Home, and from Grove House Hospital to the Royal Bath Hospital. Reports were constantly about the sick and suffering, as in this comment from a meeting of the reporter with a man in Beaulieu: 'Corporal Carrol... is suffering from the effects of gas. Carrol was asleep at the time the gas came to him and awoke to find himself suffocating...'

However, even in the climate of terrible suffering and deprivation when people were facing the most desperate hardships, the world of shops, restaurants and hotels went on. In the summer of 1917, Edward Clarke's shop on James Street still advertised 'Newest hats, model gowns, Tussore coats, wash frocks, blouses, lingerie and coloured umbrellas for sun and shower', and dances, talks, concerts and parties – many to raise money for the forces – went on as much as ever.

1918
Exhaustion and Peace

At home, early in the New Year, there was a notable ceremony of dedication to the fallen, held at Knaresborough Parish Church. The Lord Bishop of Ripon presided and, as the reporter commented: 'The shrine contains the names of all Knaresborough men who have joined His Majesty's forces during the war.' On a great, splendid brass plate there was a special tribute to a soldier and flying ace: Lieutenant David Gibson Turnbull, 'Black Watch and Royal Flying Corps'. This was especially poignant because he had died, as did so many flyers, while training at home. It was almost as if there was a particular need on that February day to pause, take a breath, and bring to mind the ones who had given their lives.

Towards the end of March in this year the Germans began their massive advance known as Operation MICHAEL. The generals had reinforced their lines on the Western Front with half a million men from the Eastern Front and now they went forward, using everything they had in their armoury, including gas and air power along with the usual big guns. Against them, initially, was a ragbag of men from all kinds of units, and they were known as Carey's Force as they were led by General Carey. This major engagement of the last year of the war was to include such celebrated locations as Beaumont Hamel, Lys and the Fourth Battle of Ypres.

Neil Gregor, summarizing the situation, put it like this: 'Victory

A manuscript diary entry from a soldier of the West Riding Territorials.
(Harrogate Central Library)

seemed in reach for the Kaiser's armies. Even as the Germans faced grinding hunger at home and at the front – the consequences of the brutally effective Allied naval blockade – they roused themselves for the Ludendorff offensive...' The German advance was backed by a bombardment of 4,600 artillery pieces and then seven divisions went forward across a front extending for 10 miles. By June, the Germans had lost 125,000 men. They were facing strong opposition from French and American troops.

One officer who would have been there but for his ill health was the poet Wilfred Owen of the Manchester Regiment. At this time he was based in Ripon, and as well as writing some of his most successful poems there at a terraced cottage in Borrage Lane, he was trying to get himself physically fit again so that he could return to the fight. He was destined to do just that, but he would be killed just a few weeks before the Armistice. However, in March and April in Ripon, he had entertainment as well. The south camp at Ripon, on Hellwath Common, was virtually a self-sufficient town, having most of the amenities and utilities of a large urban centre.

It also had a Garrison Theatre and playing there when Owen arrived was the Benson Company, who he loved. They were presenting *The Merry Wives of Windsor*, which had drawn a record crowd in Manchester and which showed off Frank Benson's talents to great effect. Benson was there at that time, because we know that he asked Owen to come and meet the company. Owen noted in a letter: 'I am going round to be introduced to B and Lucy Benson.' Benson served in the French ambulance unit in the war but clearly he was touring with his theatre company for part of the year. Owen would have had a treat. Hesketh Pearson, who knew Benson and who saw his productions, wrote: 'Everyone felt that Shakespeare was safe in the hands of one who could play cricket, tennis, football and hockey so well... and who would break the ice and enjoy a swim between a matinee of *Hamlet* and an evening performance of *Richard III*.'

Theatres played a valuable part in keeping up wartime morale, of course, but there was more to it than simply using the music halls to present patriotic songs. L.J. Collins explains the nature of theatres at the time: 'Theatre was much more than a diversionary and escapist tactic employed to provide temporary relief; indeed, the theatrical profession, in order to justify its existence, had to produce a theatre

A playbill from a Garrison Theatre production. (Author's own)

that was seen to be purposeful and relevant...' Owen certainly enjoyed the theatre at Ripon and he had seen Benson's productions before.

He was very much involved in the theatrical entertainments and even knew one of the actors, as he wrote in a letter in March: 'So strolled into the town and was just going into the cathedral when I met Isaacson the actor. He is now very much the Actor, having been discharged from Craiglockhart [a military hospital]. Benson is giving *The Merry Wives of Windsor* in the Garrison Theatre tonight.'

In the memoirs of Lady Benson she gives an account of touring in France as well, for the French troops, and she provides an interesting contrast:

> Our term of work was over in June 1917 and we returned to England, to start again with our touring company, but the unrestfulness of war had got hold of us, and we returned to France in 1918. F.R.B to drive an ambulance and I to work among the British Tommies at Étaples... It was interesting, as work among the soldiers was bound to be, but the British were much better looked after, and did not require the little comforts that the poilu was so badly in need of...

J.C. Trewin, the theatre historian, has written of Benson's Garrison Theatre enterprise in the war:

> His performances were ghosts of his former virility. Nevertheless, those Garrison Theatre tours were a terrific success. His delight at this sudden flare-up of interest was rather touching, for it was not his performance that drew the men. It was partly the magic of Shakespeare and partly, I fear, relief from the intolerable boredom of infantry training.

In early May Owen reported on more theatre visits when writing to his mother but he had been disappointed: 'Have been to two of Hall Cain's plays this week. How badly written they were!... I can recommend to you *Tides* by John Drinkwater.'

Owen's first impressions of the camp were not favourable. He sent a postcard home with the message: 'An awful camp – huts – dirty blankets – in fact WAR once more.' He shared his hut space with

Frank Benson, the actor-manager who worked with his company at the Garrison Theatre. (Author's own)

thirteen other officers and he wrote: '13 too many. Most of them are privates and sergeants in masquerade... I'd prefer to be amongst honest privates than these snobs.' Owen's recent biographer summarizes Owen's poor health after he arrived: 'Sweating under muddy, bloodstained blankets in an isolation hut, he was afraid that his 1913 illness had returned, until the doctor assured him he had caught an infection that often struck down newcomers to the camp.'

At that time there was a widespread epidemic of influenza and Owen thought he might have caught that virus, but the doctor put him right and soon Owen was walking the country around the camp, in between demanding physical exercise. He also visited Ripon Cathedral and paid some visits around Ripon and Harrogate. He found the latter 'dull' and also provided some thoughts on a local social call for his diary entry which was critical: 'Mrs Aslin can click the piano quite quickly... I wonder these people buy pianos at all, when a typewriter is so much cheaper, and makes almost the same noise.'

Owen comes across down the years as a supercilious, finicky commentator on his social world. He was unhappy for all kinds of reasons. However, his poetry came first and he found the cottage – 7 Borrage Lane – which was to be his hideaway and the place where his creativity could flower. It was here, at the little house in Ripon, that he wrote many of his most successful poems dealing with the war experience he had known. By that point, he had met Siegfried Sassoon and been at Craiglockhart Hospital in Edinburgh where his writing received the boost of Sassoon's conversations on the art.

Wilfred Owen. (wikicommons)

By April this year he had written such masterpieces as *Greater Love*, *Exposure* and *Futility*.

Before Borrage Lane, he had visited How Hill Tower, also known as the Chapel of Saint Michael De Monte, which was part of the Studley Royal estate. This was a chantry chapel, built around 1200, and was a ruin until John Aislabie developed his Studley garden plans. When Owen visited, it had been in use as a cluster of farm outbuildings since its use as a gaming house stopped in the mid eighteenth century.

Owen toyed with the idea of living there, writing this entry in his diary:

> It arrested attention as all such towers do, and I climbed up, and finding inhabitants in it, desired tea of them. Only half of the old chapel is occupied by peasants; the other is vacant. The rent would be about 2s a week! I wish it weren't so far from here. The windows have a marvellous view (for this part of the world) and I could spend my spring evenings very pleasantly up there.

There are strong hints there about Owen's negative attitudes to the wild side of Yorkshire and to the country people. It could almost be a diary of a snooty aristocrat who finds the 'peasants' there as servants ('I desired tea of them'). In his letters home, he gave some valuable insights into life at Ripon, although his comments were sometimes reserved: 'I send you a rather well-composed photograph of the village-city. You'll see that it's quite pleasant, though not beautiful.' He did get to know the environs reasonably well, though, as he walked a good deal: 'Ripon is only a mile from my hut, and through Borrage Lane... it is an interesting walk – especially this morning when the buds all make a special spurt between dawn and noon, and all the lesser celandines opened out together.' In late April he even went to Aldborough to see the Roman remains and managed to be more complimentary than usual about his Yorkshire surroundings: 'I am much too footsore to walk back so I am now waiting for a train to take me back to Harrogate. The weather is superb and I have spent an afternoon of great elation in these fine old villages.'

After the first months, Owen came to quite enjoy Ripon Camp life. He notes that there were musical performances and the facilities clearly improved. He was even given some local contacts, including people who would feed him tea and food and generally look after him.

Then, in May, he was fit again. The Medical Board considered him to be fit for service and he was ordered back to his post; he was bound for Scarborough, to join the Manchester Regiment Reserve at their base. His final destination was France and there he was to win the Military Cross, but he was killed on the Sambre Canal with the end of hostilities just a week away. Ironically, a former pupil at Ripon Grammar School, Samuel Cartwright, died the day after Owen on 5 November. A letter he wrote to an old school friend survives, and as Samuel was in the Royal Army Medical Corps, he gives us an insight into the medical work done in those horrendous conditions when he was working with an ambulance, bringing back casualties from the dressing stations. He wrote:

Well, the majority of the bearers are either working in the trenches, clearing to the two dressing stations, or else in the dressing stations themselves. These are really the first places of shelter for the wounded, and are usually small farms or buildings, where the injured are taken, and there they are looked after by our men until the ambulance arrives ready to convey them further back, perhaps three or four miles to a field hospital, although a field hospital consist of two long sheds, and this is where I am at present.

One intriguing footnote to Owen's time in Ripon is provided by Dr Roger Kendall, who has investigated the setting and references of Owen's poem *The Schoolmistress*. Dr Kendall has located the building that would have been a private girls' school in 1918, with windows facing the pavement. Owen would have passed this place many times; it is close to his Borrage Lane cottage. In fact, the teacher in question was Sarah Jane Aslin and Owen referred to a Mrs Aslin playing music in one of his letters home. This is the family of Robert Aslin, who was discussed in Chapter Two (1915). The poem has the lines:

> There, while she heard the classic lines repeat,
> Once more the teacher's face clenched stern;
> For through the window, looking on the street,
> Three soldiers hailed her. She made no return.
> One was called 'Orace whom she would not greet.

There are today, at a time when centenaries loom large, accounts of losses from particular institutions, firms or families and one such example is in Ruth Savage's account of young men from Ripon Grammar School who lost their lives in the war. She gives accounts of several scholars and their fate, including that of Samuel Cartwright.

Samuel was writing to a fellow member of the Ripon Grammar School cricket team and he notes at the end of his letter that he had 'seen Barnie' and 'met Evans twice'. There is a wonderfully boyish and cheery note to the letter and it reminds the modern reader that these young men had, in a sense, moved their camaraderie from the school playing field to the theatre of war, exactly as in Sir Henry Newbolt's famous poem in which we have the lines 'Play up, play up, and play the game.' Samuel died of wounds close to the end of the war, as already mentioned.

Ruth Savage's article includes a picture of the school cricket team as it was on the eve of war in 1913. Her comment sums up the tragedy: 'A year after this photograph was taken, Britain was at war and at least 15 out of the 16 boys went off to fight. Five never returned.' James Jameson died at Thiepval in 1916; John Tilston was killed in action in

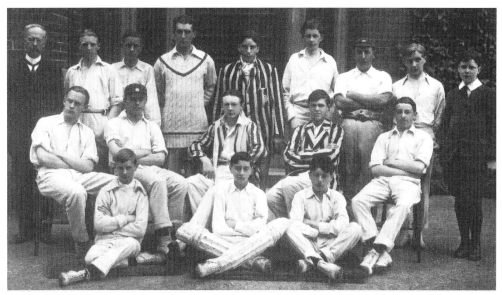

The Ripon Grammar School cricket team of 1913. (Ripon Grammar School)

Cricketer John Stanley Morton. (Ripon Grammar School)

1917; John Morton died in August 1918; and Frederick Southwell was killed in action in 1917. Their pictures show handsome, strong young men: gentlemen, sportsmen and scholars, the best of their generation, believing in honour and in the greatness of their native land.

The year 1918 will always be a date associated with the global influenza pandemic. On top of all the suffering of the war, there came a savage onslaught of this deadly infection. It began in the second half of the year and the British death toll would be around a quarter of a million people; worldwide the death toll ran into many, many millions. It is almost impossible to imagine what the emergence of the disease did to morale and to that strong resolve which had seen folk through the worst of the massive conflict. Reading about 1918, the modern student of history casting an eye over these war years will find the strain of the demand on his or her sense of empathy severely tested.

What was this terrible flu? People were familiar with it because there had been outbreaks in recent times: in 1900, 1908 and even in 1915, when health and strength were particularly in demand. Commonly known as Spanish flu, that name is something of a misnomer as the virus did not originate from Spain. Press censorship in the war years meant that no mention of it appeared in Britain and elsewhere, and the first reported cases were in neutral Spain where such censorship was not implemented.

This particularly deadly virus was a horrible, fast-acting scourge of life and wellbeing, with its warning signs of sweating, headaches and pains along the back and in the eyes. Even worse, it sent the victim's mood down low, into depression and world-weariness. Unusually for flu, which normally worst affects the very young, the elderly and those with weakened immune systems, this strain specifically attacked previously healthy young adults. Now, in 1918, it was percolating through the ranks of the young men returning home from the trenches. It then incubated in all kinds of places, from picture houses to markets and public transport or wherever crowds gathered.

Juliet Nicolson, writing about the aftermath of war, describes the infection:

> When the virus first appeared in the summer of 1918, it produced only the old familiar indicators, including sweats, headaches, pain in the eyes, back and limbs. But unusually these signs were followed by a sense of immense depression and at this stage the flu became unrecognizable from previous incarnations.

To make matters worse, there was an acute shortage of medical professionals, from nurses through to doctors. The health advisers who were available at the very top, from whence advice was sought, could offer nothing except the efficacy of alcohol and sleep. The flu took its victims in an agonizing manner, basically filling their lungs and full respiratory system with liquid – some of this being the patient's own blood – and effectively drowning them. Desperation set in as well. As Juliet Nicolson pointed out: 'Older people were accustomed to warding off illness and used their own remedies. Opium, rhubarb, treacle, laudanum, vinegar and quinine were all thought to have their own special curative powers.'

There was a reign of terror that summer, aside from the war. Children had a rhyme:

> I had a little bird
> Its name was Enza.
> I opened the window
> And in flew Enza.

It was in 1918 that the influenza pandemic struck and it would rival trench warfare in terms of the sheer, depressing statistics of death. In all parts of the land, melancholy stories relating to deaths from the flu were recorded. In Harrogate, one of the most heart-rending tales was recently unearthed by Rosemary Johnson and reported in a feature by Dan Windham. This concerns Wilhelmina Little and Lieutenant Charles Gibbon, who were married in Ripon on 11 September 1917 but were destined to enjoy just a year of marriage. The bride was to die of the flu in October 1918 and Charles died, winning the Distinguished Service Medal, in his last heroic fight while in command of the *Ariadne* on trawler patrol in the North Sea. Even with serious injuries, Charles fought on. He died in a nursing home in Falmouth on 29 October 1918. Gibbon had had a distinguished career, having been trained on HMS *Worcester* and then worked for the White Star Line. He was commissioned and served first on the *Vagrant*.

There was also the question of the returning prisoners of war. Since the declaration of war back in August 1914, there had been Harrogate and Ripon men held in internment camps at a number of places including Doberitz, Giessen and Ruhleben, the latter being around 10 kilometres from Berlin. We are not short of descriptions of these places. Escapee J.L. Hardy provided one which is very accurate, describing Magdeburg:

> There was a great deal of barbed wire, wide neutral zones, something like thirty sentry posts, and the whole place at night was ablaze with arc lamps. The spot that drew us was a little triangular courtyard behind the Wagenhaus – the building in

which we slept. We could look down into it from one of the windows... The camp orderlies were allowed to use this yard as a drying ground for washing, but no officer prisoner was allowed there, as a sentry was posted there day and night... There wasn't a chance of scaling the double wire entanglement...

The treatment of prisoners was governed by the Geneva Convention and it appears that the German authorities kept to the rules in most cases: mail was allowed to be delivered, and cultural and sporting activities were encouraged. In effect, what happened was that the camp had generated its own cultural life. One account of the place stresses the purposeful activities:

The camp detainees arranged their own entertainment. Life at the camp was so monotonous, to relieve the boredom culture flourished everywhere. There were literature classes for Grimsby fishermen, language classes, artists' clubs, domino games with home-made chips and inmates shared their reading material. Plays were produced and concerts arranged. One musician later became conductor of the Toronto Symphony Orchestra.

However, Ruhleben certainly wasn't paradise. It was still a prison, in spite of all the apparent enjoyment and community spirit. One online commentary points out that 'Personal accounts published later gave widely varying pictures of what then ensued. Some speak of hostility from the Germans, and others of compassion.'

One very full account of the Ruhleben experience comes from the skipper of the *St Cuthbert*, John Green. He explains that a U-boat came alongside and guns were pointed at him and his crew. They were forced off their ship, being given five minutes to gather their things. They were taken below and, as the night went on, three more trawler crews were taken onto the sub.

Green experienced the hulks. He wrote:

During the whole time not a piece of soap was given to us to wash ourselves, and the ship was practically covered with lice and other vermin. It was not an uncommon sight to see lice on the table and on the rails of the ship... the condition of the ship

Giessen Camp. (Harrogate Advertiser)

was heartbreaking, and try as we could we could not keep clear of the vermin.

Green managed to have an interview with the American consul, and from him he had some cash so he could buy things to improve the life of himself and his crew a little. They were at first kept at the naval barracks in Cuxhaven and conditions improved a little. However, when Green and others finally left for Ruhleben, he made a point of noting the fate of those who were unable to take the prison life:

> One old fellow, I shall never forget... when we left the hulks he was laid on the bunk, too ill to get up and should have been sent to hospital, but he was told to dress and come with us, and the dreary ride, and the only attention he received was from his comrades, was too much for him and he died soon after reaching our destination.

Recreational facilities were impressive. There was even a football league with two divisions; a camp magazine carried a page of adverts, one telling inmates that Mr Pearce of Barrack 2, Loft, offered elocution lessons; and one could have a 'first class pedicure' with George Teger, who was a 'professional coiffeur'. It could have been a holiday camp, one might think. Nevertheless, of course, beneath all this recreation and sport, there was the fact that the men were prisoners and they were cut off from home and family.

The *Harrogate Advertiser* of 10 April 1915 listed several local men as being at Ruhleben:

> Among the men... are the following: Anderson, F., Blossomgate, Ripon, barrack 10, loft; Gatliff, W., c/o Mr Hutchinson, solicitor, Ripon, 'tea-house'; Atkinson, J.I., Inglecroft, Huby, Weeton, barracks, 12. A Yorkshiremen's Society has been formed among the prisoners interned at Ruhleben Camp. The Foreign Office announces a number of improvements that have lately been carried out in the conditions of the camp and the treatment of prisoners.

The Spanish flu hit the camp, as it did everywhere else, in 1918. The field hospital tried to cope but the situation was desperate, of course. Then came the end of the war and it was time to go home. The camp captain, Joseph Powell, sorted out the process of arranging for repatriation. On 22 November the first party of men moved off, on course for home. The journey, by train, was from Rgen to Copenhagen and then there was a transfer to board a Danish ship, at least in one man's memoir, the SS *Frederick VIII*, and from there it was back to the Humber.

Many men from around Harrogate and Ripon found that their destination as prisoners was Doberitz, the first of the prisoner-of-war camps created in Germany. A picture from the *Herald* shows a group of local men at Doberitz, featuring Lance Corporal J.T. Annakin and other unnamed men. There is quite a lot to be learned about the camp from this report:

> He was captured... and sent to Doberitz, which was the first prisoners' camp established in Germany, and where most of the 1914 men were confined. They were set to do almost useless work and were fed on cabbage water and mangold-wurzels, with a small ration of black bread. The greatest complaint of the British against the Germans is that although they had plenty of food in the early part of the war, they refused to give it to prisoners.... In December he was sent to Dyrotz and was employed... censoring parcels.

Annakin added that he had at one time been ill and he said he went to a hospital where he received every consideration. Reports also showed the richness of the leisure element in Doberitz, which compared well to Ruhleben. A picture of the 'Prisoners' Association Football Club' was in the *Advertiser* in January 1916, showing Lance Corporal Gill who was the subject of much commentary at the time as he had been reported missing.

However, there were also tales of brutality. In the *Advertiser* of 18 January 1918, the following report concerned the treatment of Lance Corporal Vollans, adopted son of Mr Petch of Regent Avenue, Harrogate:

> Contracting diphtheria, Vollans was in hospital for six weeks. There was no medicine and the patients had to take their luck. Whilst going to work, one vicious old Boche would kick the prisoners' ankles if he thought they were not going quickly enough, many of them being too weak to walk. At length the French arrived and brought relief, and Vollans was in hospital again, and was well looked after...

If we look for a truly dramatic story from the prisoners' tales, this can be found in abundance regarding Harold Welborn of Harrogate. While escorting a prisoner during the 1918 big push of the enemy, he himself was caught and taken to face some officers at a dugout. When they wanted to see his gas mask they found a map inside, which he had taken as a souvenir as it was a German one. The officers found him most suspicious and decided he was a spy, so he was to be shot. The firing squad was to be carried out at six the next day and he was escorted away, along with a wounded German whom he had escorted earlier. The *Advertiser* concludes the story:

> At length the wounded man had to rest and he and the Harrogate youth sat down on a bank by the roadside... the two German guards got the wind up... leaving Welborn and the wounded German... Taking advantage of the situation, Welborn retraced his steps... and took shelter in a recess in the rocks. Hardly had they done so than a body of Germans was heard moving... the wounded man, who could have summed his fellow-soldiers, whispered 'Hush'... When daylight came Seaman Welborn piloted the wounded man to a medical unit and rejoined his battalion...

Naturally, in most cases very little was heard from the prisoners. A typical example would be the case of George Graham of the 2nd KOYLI, of King's Road, Harrogate. He was captured at Mons and taken to Doberitz. His card home is simple and minimal:

> Dear Nell – Just a couple of lines to let you know I am still living. Hope you and family are all in the best of health. I haven't had a card from you in weeks. I received a small parcel of cigs etc from the *Harrogate Advertiser*. One of them had a card with your address on. We are not allowed to send private cards. Remember me to all...

The question arose of how to treat and help the prisoners when they came home and Ripon played a key role in that. It was opined that the returned prisoners needed 'decontamination'. In Parliament the subject was discussed and this extract from a Hansard report of 20 November

1918 shows the thinking at the time, with Viscount Devonport asking the House what was being done. He gave his opinion:

> I have seen in the papers that it is contemplated, as released prisoners arrive, to intern them in some sort of prisoners' camp. As regards those that are combatant prisoners, members of the Army, I see no objection to that... But I think that the Government will find that if they attempt to intern returned civilians there will be the greatest possible resistance to it, and that it will be a most unpopular move. Their great desire will be to get home and see their families, from whom they have been severed for these four dreary years...

Lord Newton explained what had been done regarding the reception camps, and Ripon was in those plans: 'If they elect to be treated as combatants they will, of course, go to two large rest camps of which I spoke the other day – namely at Ripon and Dover; and they will, after being detained there for as short a time as possible, be returned to their homes...'

Women's lives were changing apace, of course. The franchise was extended this year and women over 30 who met the minimum property qualifications were given the vote, giving this right to 8.4 million women. In March there was a real sign of the times when, just down the road in Keighley, Nina Boyle, who had long been active in the Women's Freedom League, told the press that she intended to stand for Parliament in the Keighley by-election. One report commented: 'It is not clear whether women now have the right to stand for parliament, but she wishes to settle the matter by a test case. It is probable that several other women will follow her example.'

The Armistice eventually came, of course, and it was time for the whole country to take a deep breath, look around and gather together whatever could be retrieved in that vast array of broken lives. In the limbo between the shock and elation of the end of hostilities, there came a dark side. Sir Patrick Hastings, the great lawyer, expressed this powerfully and he wrote from close knowledge of the criminal world he had known in his work in the London courts: 'The country was overrun by a horrible breed of profiteers who had made immense fortunes throughout the war; no reasonable attempt seemed to have been made by Mr Lloyd George or his government to stop them...'

The civilian efforts all across the home front had been gargantuan, principally in committing time, effort and resolution to the success of agricultural production, maintaining food supplies during the sea blockades and U-boat attacks. In the midst of the Second World War, the *Countryman* magazine reminded readers of the triumphs and achievements of the Land Army in the Great War:

In August, 1918 a survey was taken of 12,637 Land Army members. The returns included 5,734 milkers, 293 tractor-drivers, 3,971 field workers, 635 carters, 260 ploughmen, 84 thatchers, and 21 shepherds. Can we doubt that with the extension of physical fitness, the development of motor-driving, and every kind of outdoor sport, members of the present Women's Land Army are capable of surpassing the pioneers?

In May this year there was a high-level celebration of the work of the Women's Land Army with an open-air meeting on the Stray on Saturday, 18 May. A great procession of workers walked from Station Square headed by the band of A Company, 15th Battalion West Riding Volunteer Regiment. The press added a very Yorkshire comment: 'If wet, the meeting will be held in the Winter Gardens.' The real purpose was for recruiting, of course. On 22 May, the local report was:

An open air meeting was held on the West Park Stray, over which Admiral Sir Francis Bridgeman presided. He said that 30,000 agricultural labourers had to go to the front and women were asked to come forward in great numbers, to assist to cultivate the land... The Mayor (Councillor F G Johnson) said they wanted 300 recruits from Harrogate to help in agriculture. The Director of Food Production had told them that it was not at the present moment that difficulty was apprehended, but next winter, if great efforts were not made...

By the last months of the year, barely had the Armistice been agreed before the more militant workers were threatening strikes and their reasons, as given in a pamphlet published by the Clydebank Scottish Labour Party, express what must have been a general sense of discontent:

> During the war, from press and platform, it was impressed upon the workers that if they only fought and worked... and won the war, they would then see the dawn of a new era.... What a surprise the workers got. The Armistice was no sooner declared than thousands of them were thrown out of employment...

As the end of hostilities came, the news of the last of the fallen trickled in. Among them was Lance Corporal W.P. Clarke of the Sherwood Foresters, the son of Mr and Mrs W. Clarke of Knaresborough. Spending the Armistice in hospital in France, along with many others, was Private Alfred Smith of the 10th West Yorks. He was astoundingly unfortunate in that he had been wounded four times and also gassed.

CHAPTER 6

1919
The Aftermath

When a war such as the Great War comes to an end and people are left with memories, time tends to shift perspectives and it is with the memorabilia of the events of those four years that we have to deal. Sometimes, the documentation of the years immediately after 1918 provides evidence that some folk wanted to rub out the horrendous experience forever. Such a family story was printed in the *Harrogate Advertiser* in March 2015 when, in a feature on Stanley Crossley's letters home to his beloved, the author Dan Windham noted, quoting Stan Beer: 'When my granddad died grandmother tore the letters up and then put them in the bin. I think she did it because they were quite private memories and she did not want to be reminded of them.'

More generally and powerfully, in one oral history archive relating to Bradford, one woman tells the interviewer, referring to the news of mass deaths from the Somme when a whole street lost its young men: 'After that, my mother never went to church again, and she believed in nothing.'

Looking for the human stories and developing their significance is always productive. Go to any local school magazine or church parish magazine of the war years and there will be groups and lists, all relating to the casualties of the war. Ruth Savage has reported on research by the Old Rips, the former pupils' association, who investigated the 1913 Ripon Grammar School cricket team in this way and provided a profile of each young man, touching on war experience and also other career details. This is a powerful and effective way to see the reality of the war and its knock-on effects in every other walk of life. Ruth Savage's comments give a fascinating profile of what was surely a typical situation across the country. For instance: 'Of the 287 former RGS pupils and teachers who fought in the first world war just over 80%, including many injured, returned home. The impact on such a small school community must have been immense.'

The list of deaths makes solemn reading: James Jameson, aged 20, died at the Somme on the second day of the battle; John Tilston was a second lieutenant in the Machine Gun Corps and was killed on 23 April 1917; Frederick Southwell was killed on 10 April 1917, and so on.

In the first months of the year, the most prominent issue was how, when and where to demob the thousands of troops returning home. Technically, when the men had signed their attestation certificates upon enlistment, they had agreed to serve a longish period after hostilities ceased. However, such contracts are not simply and logically held and controlled. There was trouble arising from frustration, slow bureaucracy and officialdom. Just before Christmas 1918, the government had tried to make some apparently sensible moves towards helping with this process. They created a 'Z Class' of returnees: these were men urgently needed back in civilian life. Yet even this needed a proviso: 'As the power of recall will not be exercised except in case of military emergency, its existence will not interfere with the resettlement of the men...'

On the first day of the New Year 1919, Sir Eric Geddes, First Lord of the Admiralty, was given control of the demob system. *The Times* gave some figures of the numbers of people involved: 'The Navy, the Army and the Air Force, numbered at the beginning of the Armistice, 6,500,000 men. But the total war effort of the country at home and abroad, in terms of man-power and woman-power, exceeded 10,000,000 persons.' At that date, 775,000 people had already been released.

There was also the question of the returned prisoners of war, so all those Harrogate and Ripon men who had been in the German camps were subject to a specific process of repatriation. One body assisting with this was the Government Committee on the Treatment by the Enemy of British Prisoners of War. Robert Younger at the Royal Courts of Justice outlined what was going to happen, explaining that the committee's representatives would go to 'the dispersal camps at Dover and at Ripon, there... to receive from every returned prisoner of war information... of which the knowledge of the Committee is incomplete...' In other words, more officialdom to slow things down.

Regarding the men at Ripon, statistics issued in November 1918 were that 444 officers and 8,458 other ranks arrived at Ripon late that month and *The Times* reported that 'Three officers and 5,838 other ranks have arrived at Ripon this week from Germany, Holland, Denmark and Norway...'

It was also a time for awards, at least by the time the dust had settled and everyone began taking stock of achievements within the great theatre of war, both at home and abroad. The medical professionals (and amateurs) were well-deserving of recognition, of course, and in the case of the Australian Assistant Matron Cecilia Harries there was the significant award of the Royal Red Cross. She was working with the Queen Alexandra's Imperial Military Nursing Service Reserve at their hospital in Ripon. The QAIMNSR had been established in 1902, replacing the old Army Nursing Service, and these awards were central to their work, being given for 'exceptional service in military nursing'.

One significant story of the war, with regard to Ripon and the camps, came to a head in 1919. This was the Canadian Khaki University, and if we glance at Private Percy Adams' war we can see how this educational initiative fits into the larger scheme of things. Percy joined the 15th Battalion Canadian Infantry in February 1918. In October he was attached to burial parties. Then he was given leave and came to England. He had been part of the Central Ontario Regiment but found himself at Ripon Camp between February and May. In that period he attended classes of the Khaki University before boarding the SS *Baltic*, heading for home, in early summer. He was a typical beneficiary of this wonderful scheme, first begun at the front by the Chaplain Service and the YMCA and known there as the University of Vimy Ridge.

In late 1915, this educational provision for troops on active service was largely run by the chaplaincy. An academic called Oliver was given the rank of honorary captain in the 196th Western Universities Battalion and one of his tasks was educational work. By early 1917 the Canadian YMCA and the chaplains, led by Oliver, were pressing for formal recognition for their organization. Dr Tory of the University of

Officers of the Canadian Khaki University. (Springfield College)

Alberta came to visit and report on what was happening at the front and he recommended the setting-up of a group to be known as the Khaki College of Canada.

From this the whole notion burgeoned and, as Jack Coggins has written: 'The embryonic Khaki College of Canada would offer courses in secondary high school subjects leading to matriculation and entrance prerequisites into Canadian and British Universities. Oliver's task was to transform the idea into an institution.' The name Vimy Ridge was first used because the Canadians had distinguished themselves in a victory there in April 1917.

The Khaki University took off. It was to have two semesters, running between October 1918 and May 1919, and as well as basic literacy there were to be foreign language classes, commerce and agriculture on the curriculum. Certificates were issued and all seemed well. That was until demobilization. It was going to take a long time for this process to be carried through. Also, the principle of 'first in, first out' was not adhered to. There were demob riots, particularly at Kinmel Camp on Anglesey. After that trouble, the work towards repatriation became rather more streamlined. Meanwhile, the teaching and learning went on and there were to be several Khaki College centres in British camps, while Ripon was designated the central base in England. One historian has summarized the situation at Ripon:

> The students remained at Ripon until the Khaki University was closed in June 1919 as the last of the men were shipped home to Canada to resume their former lives. The Khaki University and its colleges had lasted less than two years, during which time about fifty thousand men registered to take courses and about a thousand of them received educational credits for a year of regular college work.

The classes were intended to reduce the boredom in the camps, of course, but there were genuine benefits, as shown by the above figures. In May 1919 *The Times* had a special correspondent at Ripon and in their report we have the following:

> The Khaki University of Canada is established in the great South Camp at Ripon. There passes through the camp a constant stream of men homeward bound, and yet in these surroundings of excitement and change the students of the University maintain a settled and tranquil life. They have made a calm oasis in an area of perpetual restlessness. Amid the parade of arms and so close to the drilling grounds that the words of command invade the open windows of their lecture-rooms, they have discovered a way to seclude themselves with their textbooks on the arts and sciences.... The only premises are wooden huts of the type which have been the Army's lodging-places from the time when the nation applied itself seriously to the business of soldiering... private study is impossible...

The whole enterprise had begun through sheer force of will and by people reaching deep into their pockets. Professor Henry Oliver wrote home to his wife: 'I'm spending what money I can afford on the hospitals and reading rooms... I have got together, to a great extent through purchase, a fair library again.' Dr Tory, who surveyed the whole scheme, pointed out the obvious benefits: 'There is no doubt in the minds of the military authorities that such educational work... would be of great benefit to the soldiers from the point of view of military efficiency and general morale...' He had understood that boredom, as well as the enemy, needed to be defeated.

During the period from July 1918 to May 1919 there was a story from the Ripon camps that had begun as a small scrap of military discipline, yet had ended in the high courts of justice. It has become a key case in the legal study of tort – a wrong (or alleged wrong) done to a person – but in this instance done while the plaintiff was in the army and subject to army regulations.

There must have been grievances, omissions, jealousies and burning resentment for all kinds of reasons in a space in which thousands of men were placed together to train as fighters in a world war. Human relations are always problematic and arguably more so in wartime conditions. Add to that the accumulation of 'citizen soldiers' and volunteers mixed with the regular, professional army and the stage is set for all varieties of conflict. This case, begun at Ripon, is known as Heddon v Evans.

Christopher Heddon was a solicitor, practising in Harrogate and Ripon, and he enlisted in the Royal Army Service Corps (known with humour as 'Ally Sloper's Cavalry') which dealt with matters of transport and what today would be called 'logistics'. Mr Heddon was a mere private at the time. In mid-1918, his wife being seriously ill with diphtheria and probably also with the influenza virus, Heddon asked for leave to visit her. When this was refused and Heddon allegedly went to her bedside without permission, he was charged with desertion and sentenced to fifteen days CB (confined to barracks). Heddon said that two letters in which he complained of the injustice of being falsely imprisoned had gone missing, and that there was no reason why he could not have made the visit because 'his day's work consisted in striking a match at 8 a.m. and lighting the incinerator.'

The result was that Heddon took out an action against his commanding officer, Major Evans, for false imprisonment. In fact, Heddon had been kept at a military prison in Fulford, York and there had been no occasion for him to make a plea or state a case. The assumption was that he would wait to face a court martial, the inference being that he was presumed guilty.

This led to the employment of barristers and eventually to the High Court of Justice in May 1919. During the intervening period, while cases were being prepared, Mrs Heddon died (in February 1919). Mr Justice McCardie heard the case on 2 May. The prosecution argued that Heddon had experienced detention, not arrest in barracks; they argued that the regulations in the King's Regulations handbook had not been adhered to and so a conflict emerged between the law generally and the minutiae of military law. The following interchange summed up the impasse:

> HIS LORDSHIP: Is there nothing in the Army Code defining the rights of the private soldier?
> Mr T. ATKINSON: There is not as far as I am yet aware.

In fact, at one point the judge questioned whether or not the right of habeas corpus had not been overridden by the use of army power to inflict immediate punishment. One particular interchange pointed clearly to the weakness in the military actions:

> HIS LORDSHIP: Heddon was kept at the detention barracks on a warrant which only authorized his detention for seven days. He was kept for 18 days. How do you justify that?
> WITNESS: He was awaiting court martial.
> HIS LORDSHIP: He was put outside the custody of the regiment, and there should have been a proper authority for doing so.
> MR T. ATKINSON: There is a regulation dealing with the matter.
> HIS LORDSHIP (to the witness): What is the regulation?
> WITNESS: I do not know (laughter).

In the end, it was ruled that simply because a man becomes a serviceman, he does not lose the right to appeal to the civil courts against a perceived wrong done to him. The point at issue was really that the officer had no right to apply a punishment as it was a case for a court martial. Even if the officer had had the jurisdiction, he had to give his prisoner the option of a trial by court martial since the custody involved loss of pay.

There must have been celebrations in Ripon in late May that year among Mr Heddon and his friends, although his wife's death would have cast a dark shadow over him. He had taken on the British army in a fight for individual rights and he had triumphed.

As part of the broader picture, it is meaningful to see this episode as being a product of the Defence of the Realm Act (DORA) of 1914. This led to an Order of Council known as regulation 14B by which persons 'of hostile origin or associations' might be interned without any real investigation into status. In other words, there was a common attitude of doing things as if there were emergency powers, sometimes for the smallest breaches of discipline. After all, other nations had experienced mass mutinies by troops; the fear was there within the establishment as they looked around at their neighbours.

However, as Harrogate and Ripon had, certainly by this time, been prominent in their work of helping with convalescence and medical treatment, it has to be noted that there was marked success. Harrogate was the only spa town to end the war with a healthy profit, therefore being in advance of others such as Buxton and Bath. There had been a wide variety of treatments available to recovering soldiers, and the existing photographs of this area of life show such treatments as diathermy (electro-therapy applied to the skin) being administered to troops in Harrogate. The war definitely boosted the popularity of all kinds of therapies, as extreme wounds – both of body and of mind – had forced the caring professions to apply more energy and skill to new ways of treating such maladies. The medical press through the 1920s was full of adverts promoting such treatments as 'electric ionization' and 'Physiotherapeutics'.

In fact, as research by Carol Harris has shown, physiotherapy generally as we know it today has strong links to the Great War. The Almeric Massage Corps, for instance, was created by Almeric and Pauline Paget, began with a well-trained group of fifty masseuses and given qualification by the Incorporated Society of Trained Masseuses. Carol Harris explains their work, after they became known as Almeric Paget's Military Massage Corps, with reference to the daily work of a typical masseuse:

Whether she is stimulating muscles by the use of the Bristow coil or subjecting a limb to interrupted galvanism, ionization or a Schnee bath, diathermy or radiant heat, her constant attention to every detail is essential... A masseuse will spend three months in the massage ward, and then will follow three months of electrical treatment...

Their work at the army convalescent camps has been well explained. Carol Harris uses a newspaper report from Alnwick Camp as an example and notes that 'The interior of every hut is now comfortably arranged and fitted up, and every week wounded men in a convalescent stage are arriving in the camps for treatment... The dowsing heat treatment is now in good working order and some 123 men are massaged every morning...' The masseuses worked at most of the camps across England: Olive Guthrie-Smith worked at Sleaford; Winifred Letts worked at camps in Northumberland and Manchester; and Pauline Paget created a massage department at the Miller General Hospital in Greenwich.

During the course of the war the figure for the number of men who were shot in the head or face, or who were hit in those areas by shrapnel, is around 60,000. The hospitals were consequently very busy and some sort of fluent system needed to be in place in the last year of the war as matters escalated and improved technology on the battlefield increased the vulnerability of infantrymen.

We may see the general trajectory of the treatment of casualties by looking at one example: Private Gill, a Canadian soldier. Following the Armistice he was brought back to England on 23 November and taken to Ripon, where the Central Ontario Regimental Depot was placed. From there he was sent to a convalescent camp at Whitley until January 1919, and then by early April he was on board ship, leaving Liverpool for home. It is clear from this that Ripon, being a very large-scale camp, was a frequent first stop for all categories of casualties and from there they would gradually be given more specific help. Gill, for instance, was said to have neurasthenia. It needs to be recalled at this point that by 1919, the Ripon camps had become rather a massive junction in terms of the 'traffic' of the injured and the repatriated. They would be a mix of transit camp and appraisal centre, such was the sheer, perplexing variety of illness created by the war, from 'mental cases' to broken limbs and from prisoners of war to internees.

First-hand accounts give us particular insights. Dr P.R. Liddle, for instance, wrote the following to show the hardihood and courage of the men from around Leeds, whose letters are now preserved in the Liddle Collection at Leeds University:

> I would like to take these letter extracts... First, 'Myself I seem to be hit all over. 14 wounds to the left leg, 2 in the right thigh and 2 in the wrist and a scratch on the forehead. Otherwise I am quite alright....' Second, 'When I came round and saw my leg I thought the surgeon had mistaken it for a leg of mutton...' and third, 'This is just a line to let you know I have got wounded. It was a rifle grenade that did it. It isn't at all serious so don't worry. I got two holes in my right leg...'

Dr Liddle added in this essay that he carried out a survey with a set of these wounded men in 1921 and he concludes 'Not one spoke with bitterness about his loss...' The modern reader surely has to gasp in admiration and sheer wonder at this courage.

The retrospectives of 1919 also brought sensational and almost incredible stories, a variety of war narratives that astonish the reader. Such a tale was experienced by the Newbould family of Nidderdale, who had six sons enlist and they all returned home. The *Advertiser*, back in 1916, had printed a picture and a report on them, showing Shadrach, Samuel, Robert, Meshach, Tommy and Arthur. Four of the men joined up at the outbreak of war and one – Tommy, who had been in Canada – returned home to join up.

One of them, Samuel, remained in Germany for a while after 1918 but came home later. In 2014 the *Advertiser* spoke to Mrs Arrand, Samuel's daughter, and she said: 'My father never really talked about the war, he must have had difficult memories.... It wasn't until the outbreak of the Second World War that he started to talk about it.'

Remarkable stories like this came to light when people looked back and insisted on seeing positive aspects as well as bearing the inevitable mourning. Most towns and cities appear to have had their tales of large families going to war. In fact, there is another highly unusual group of brothers: Tom, Arnold and Arthur Dean. Their father was a building materials stockist in Ilkley. Arnold, who lived in Harrogate, was just 24 when war broke out; he became a lieutenant in the 5th Yorkshire Territorials and survived the war. Arthur was in the West Riding Rifles, again an officer, and moved to the 4th Battalion East Yorkshires. He was killed in action on 3 July 1917 but won the Distinguished Conduct Medal, gazetted in 1916. The other brother, Tom, was just 17 in 1914; he joined the Royal Artillery and survived the war.

Another retrospective was a French view of the Tommies; this came across in letters written by a French soldier who was in Harrogate. He wrote to the *Leeds Mercury* and said:

> I have had several occasions of meeting the British troops and chatting to them. They are behaving splendidly and are a credit to the old country. They have captured our hearts by their cheery spirit and undaunted courage and are in fact looked upon as the army of British gentlemen, whereas there is nothing too treacherous, mean, low, cruel and atrocious the German hordes stop at.

French opinions had not been too common, apart from in books written from the front in a documentary way such as Philip Gibbs' *The Soul of the War*, which follows his journeys through the lines as a correspondent.

Other notable deaths in 1919 included that of the cricketer, James Rothery, who had played 150 matches for Yorkshire between 1903 and 1910, making 4,614 runs in that period. What more cruel fate could strike such a man than having a serious arm injury? He was hit by shrapnel in January 1918 and was at Heatherdene, the hospital on Wetherby Road used by the Countess George, and the *Herald* reported that he was expected to undergo another operation. The report said:

> Members of Private Rothery's family have learnt recently that it was first practically decided when he was admitted to hospital in the South that the arm would have to come off, and then one of the doctors thought it could be saved, with the result that Private Rothery is still in possession of the limb and likely to remain so.

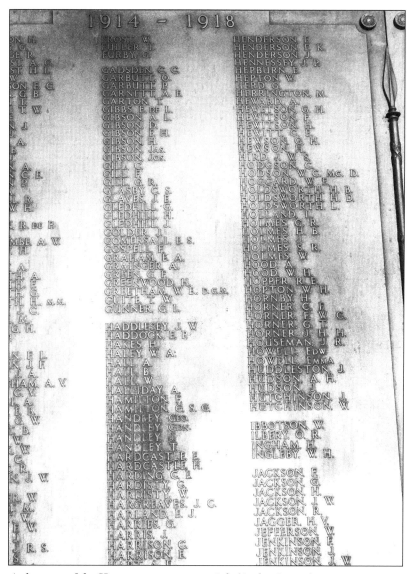

A close-up of the Harrogate war memorial. (Author's own)

Matters appeared to be optimistic at that point and the *Herald* expressed the views that everyone must have been thinking about such a talented player: what was his future likely to be in the game he loved?

They opined: 'It is full early yet to venture an opinion as to whether the erstwhile Yorkshire County cricketer will be able when the war is over to take up again an active part in league cricket – he played latterly in the Durham League – but he hopes... to act as coach...'

Sadly it was reported that, after more than a year of medical treatment and a battle to save his arm, Rothery died on 2 June 1919 at Beckett's Park Hospital in Leeds. It can only be imagined what a long and agonizing final eighteen months of life the young man had. It was, of course, a terrible loss for his father Joseph of Staincliffe and his mother Mrs Haley of Harrogate, but it was also a great loss to Yorkshire cricket. James had been in a Royal Fusiliers Sportsman's battalion and he was one of three celebrated Yorkshire players who perished in the war. The others were Major Booth, who had died on the first day of the Battle of the Somme, and Fairfax Gill of Wakefield, who had been shot in the head at Boulogne in November 1917. All those potentially successful sporting careers were dashed, and of the three, Rothery's presents us with the most heart-rending in that he suffered such a slow decline into death with flickers of hope along the way.

At the end of 1919, when the worst of the Spanish flu had passed and the first waves of the various returned casualties, prisoners and detainees had been dealt with, it would have been one of the great ironies of history to reflect that a local person, writing in the *Herald* on 12 August 1914, had said: 'It is difficult to realize from local conditions that England is at war. Everywhere in our town nature suggests peace.' In fact, it has been estimated, as in the Pump Room exhibition on the war running through 2014, that 879 Harrogate people had died during the course of the war.

As was the feeling across the land when people took a retrospective view, there had been a general sense of life hanging in the air from August 1914 – of a great suspension, a limbo – covering everything from Donald Bell's interrupted career with Bradford Park Avenue as full back to the lesser-known but equally tragic lives curtailed or ended, in their thousands. As several historians have pointed out, in 1919 one of the toughest experiences was actually to admit, deep down, that the lost ones left on the fields of France and Belgium were really dead and gone. For many, there had been no definite information as to where, when and how that loved one had died. Even grief and its rituals were in suspension for many. Dealing with the dead had become far more than simply arranging matters with an undertaker and a vicar. It involved distance, both geographical and emotional, and that pre-war early summer of 1914 must have seemed like a place in a distant dream, the reality of which had to be questioned.

Regarding the long aftermath of the war and its long-term effects on the combatants who tried to rebuild their lives, there was the lingering problem of how to help the servicemen with regard to a whole range of ills and sufferings. One of the first major steps in doing something really proactive in this respect came with the establishment of the Royal British Legion in 1921. As their current website explains:

> Over six million men had served in the war – 725,000 never returned. Of those who came back, 1.75 million had suffered some kind of disability and half of these were permanently disabled. To this figure then had to be added those who depended on those who had gone to war – the wives and children, widows and orphans...

There were also significant political effects and the growth of the Labour Party was marked. As Kenneth Morgan has pointed out, the electoral reforms of 1918, which brought more women into the franchise at last, also brought more workers in: '... the 1918 franchise reforms extended the electorate from about 8 million to over 21 million. This meant a huge increase in the working-class vote and the encouragement of a tendency to polarize politics on the grounds of class.' Thus that notable mixing of class within the army, which has often been remarked by students of the now celebrated war poets, now had a chance to have an effect on central power but it arguably faded in the post-war conditions of austerity and unemployment. If there had been any kind of revolution in the trenches, it had been in attitudes to war, especially imperial and technological war.

In the end, it is becoming increasingly difficult to assess the real significance of that massive, staggering loss of life caused by the war. What was it all for? We look today with what should be the wisdom of hindsight but, in fact, waves of widely influential media images and interpretations have engulfed a few basic, undeniable facts. First, beneath all the rhetoric of the call to arms and appeals for universal sacrifice – of time, life, family and future – this was a war that

The Harrogate war memorial in Prospect Square. (Author's own)

Prospect Square, not long after the memorial was erected. (Author's own)

happened because something had to stand in the way of the militaristic greed of the German Empire. As Gary Sheffield has argued, should the allied forces have lost the fight, there would have been 'a world in which Europe was dominated by a victorious German Empire that stretched from the Channel to the Ukraine in which liberal democracy' would have been 'extinguished'.

As a coda to the central narrative concerned with the war years, it must be noted that the casualties went on, long after 1918, because there was still an engagement with enemy forces in Mesopotamia (modern-day Iraq, Syria and Kuwait) and once again, with Ripon Grammar School in mind, there was an old boy lost in action on 14 February 1920. This was Lieutenant Arthur Trevithick Tyack Bake, who entered the school in 1912 and won a cadetship to the Indian army in July 1916. He died while fighting the Kurds; a strongly ironic note bearing in mind the contemporary situation in Syria with the ISIS aggression. The writer in the *Herald* at the time explained: 'Since the armistice there appears to have been considerable trouble with refractory and warlike tribes, especially the Kurds; the letters home describing these operations were particularly interesting, including the storming of a stronghold amongst the mountains at a height of 7,500 feet above sea level...'

In the *Herald* of April 1920, a letter was printed from Major C.J. Woodhouse to Arthur's father, Mr H.J. Tyack Bake of Harlow Moor Drive. The officer wrote:

> It will, I am sure, be a consolation to you in your bereavement to know how gallantly he had behaved on a number of occasions in Kurdistan, and also up the Euphrates, and on this last occasion when he met his end bringing back a Lewis gun, of which the team had been killed or wounded.

Arthur Bake. (Ripon Grammar School)

The major added that Arthur's party had been greatly outnumbered, around six or seven to one.

In the *Herald* war reporting columns, Breare gave a fuller picture of Arthur's work:

> About February 1918 he volunteered for service in Mesopotamia, and for a period of rather more than two years during his stay there to the time of his death, he was the only officer of his regiment who was never absent from duty either from illness or from any other cause. As so many other officers were from time to time incapacitated he was almost continuously 'Acting Captain' during the last 12 months. During the war period, one could only hazard conjectures as to his whereabouts, which appear to have been far distant from Baghdad...

The small but significant memorial stone to the fallen. (Ripon Grammar School)

His friend, Peter Nicholson from Leeds, added his opinion and gave a personal, warm-hearted touch to the tributes: 'Your son was very popular amongst us all and his loss, I am sure, will be deeply felt in the regiment. He did very good work during the Kurdistan operations and he was always a cheery boy to meet.'

It has to be said that Lieutenant Bake exemplified all the acknowledged virtues of the English schoolboy groomed and shaped for exemplary manhood. He appears to be the last in a long line of glorious dead in the annals of the Ripon Grammar School. The Old Riponians who fell in the war are remembered on a memorial tablet in the school library and also on a memorial stone beneath a tree in the school playing fields.

Bibliography and Sources

Note

Rather surprisingly, what I expected to be the major topics of the book – namely the hospitals and the Ripon camps – turned out to be the most elusive to explore. Consequently, much of the description of the training camp has been gleaned from existing works on the Pals battalions, and the material on the hospitals came from no central source. Once again, as so often with local history, a good deal of the most interesting and dramatic material came from memoirs, footnotes and throwaway comments. The bibliography of the Great War is huge and it is expanding daily but still, one suspects that many of the most intriguing narratives are still in the shadow of the chronology.

Primary Sources

Ackerley, J.R., *Escapers All* (London, The Bodley Head, 1922)

Barbellion, W.N.P., *The Journal of a Disappointed Man* (London, Penguin, 1948)

Benson, Lady, *Mainly Players: Bensonian Memories* (London, Thornton Butterworth, 1926)

Blatchford, Robert, *Germany and England: The War that was Foretold* (London, *Daily Mail*, 1915)

Buchan, John, *The Battle of the Somme: First Phase* (London, Thomas Nelson, 1919)

Bunting, Madeleine, *The Plot* (London, Granta, 2009)

Chapman, Guy (ed.), *Vain Glory: A Miscellany of the Great War* (London, Cassell, 1937)

Charman, Terry, *The First World War on the Home Front* (London, André Deutsch, 2014)

Coggins, Jack, *A Chaplain's War: Edmund Henry Oliver and the*

University of Vimy Ridge 1916–1919 (This text sourced from University of Saskatchewan archives: Essays Vol. 3, No. 1, 2004)

Corelli, Marie, *Patriotism or Self-Advertisement?* (London, Greening & Co., 1900)

Davies, Jane, *The York and Lancaster Regiment* (Stroud, Tempus, 2000)

De Groot, Gerard, *Back in Blighty* (London, Vintage Books, 2014)

Ferguson, Norman, *The First World War: A Miscellany* (Chichester, Summersdale, 2014)

Fountain, Nigel (ed.), *When the Lamps Went Out* (London, Guardian Books, 2014)

Gott, Jim, *Bits & Blots of t'Owd Spot* (Thirsk, author, 1987)

Graham, John W., *Conscription and Conscience: A History 1916–1919* (London, George Allen and Unwin, 1922)

Grand Duchess Marie of Russia, *Things I Remember* (London, Cassell, 1930)

Haber, Dr L.F., *Gas Warfare 1915–1945* (London, Bedford College, 1976)

Halliday, Paul D., *Habeas Corpus* (Cambridge, Massachusetts, Harvard University Press, 2010)

Hastings, Sir Patrick, *Autobiography* (London, Heinemann, 1948)

Healey, Denis, *My Secret Planet* (London, Penguin, 1992)

Hooper, Colette, *Railways of the Great War with Michael Portillo* (London, Transworld, 2014)

Isherwood, Christopher, *Kathleen and Frank* (London, Methuen, 1971)

Jones, Nigel, *Rupert Brooke: Life, Death and Myth* (London, Richard Cohen, 1999)

Kerr, Gordon, *A Short History of the First World War* (Harpenden, Pocket Essentials, 2014)

Kevill, Martin (ed.), *The Personal Diary of Nurse de Trafford 1916–1920* (Lewes, The Book Guild, 2001)

Mappen, Ellen, *Helping Women at Work: The Women's Industrial Council 1889–1914* (London, Hutchinson, 1985)

McCrery, Nigel, *The Final Season* (London, Random House, 2014)

Morton, D.S., *The 40 Hours Strike* (Glasgow, Clydebank S.L.P., 1918)

Neesam, Malcolm, *Harrogate* (Stroud, Nonsuch, 1995)

Neesam, Malcolm, *Hotel Majestic* (Harrogate, Paramount Hotels, 2000)

Newbury, Maggie, *Reminiscences of a Bradford Mill Girl* (Bradford, City of Bradford Metropolitan Council, 1980)

Nicolson, Juliet, *The Great Silence* (London, John Murray, 2009)

O'Sullivan, Richard, *Military Law and the Supremacy of the Civil Courts* (London, Stevens & Sons, 1923)

Owen, Wilfred, *The Collected Poems of Wilfred Owen* (London, Chatto & Windus, 1968)

Pankhurst, E. Sylvia, *The Home Front* (London, Hutchinson, 1932)

Pearson, Hesketh, *The Last Actor-Managers* (London, Methuen, 1950)

Pontefract, Ella and Hartley, Marie, *Yorkshire Tour* (London, J.M. Dent, 1939)

Pope, Jessie, *Jessie Pope's War Poems* (London, Grant Richards, 1915)

Powell, Anne, *Women in the War Zone: Hospital Service in the First World War* (Stroud, The History Press, 2009)

Powell, Geoffrey and Powell, John, *The History of the Green Howards* (Barnsley, Leo Cooper, 1992)

Pratt, Edwin A., *British Railways and the Great War* (London, Selwyn & Blount, 1921)

Priestley, J.B., *English Journey* (London, Heinemann, 1994)

Priestley, J.B., *Margin Released* (London, Heinemann, 1962)

Raw, David, *Bradford Pals* (Barnsley, Pen & Sword, 2005)

Read, Herbert, *The Contrary Experience: Autobiographies* (London, Secker & Warburg, 1963)

Rogers, James, *Railways of Harrogate and District: A History* (Harrogate, author, 1986)

Sadler, John and Serdiville, Rosie, *Tommy Rot: World War 1 Poetry They Didn't Let You Read* (Stroud, The History Press, 2013)

Sheffield, Gary, *The First World War in 100 Objects* (London, André Deutsch, 2013)

The Medical Annual (Bristol, John Wright & Sons, 1923)

Thorpe's Illustrated Guide to Harrogate of 1886 (Dewsbury, Chantry Press, 1986)

Trewin, J.C., *Benson and the Bensonians* (London, Barrie & Rockliff, 1960)

Vickers, R.L., *Leeds Road and Rail* (Stroud, Sutton, 1994)

Ward Lock's Guide to Harrogate (London, Ward Lock, 1922)

Warner, Philip, *World War One: A Chronological Narrative* (London, Arms & Armour, 1995)

Wilkinson, Roni, *Pals on the Somme 1916* (Barnsley, Pen & Sword, 2006)

Yapp, K.V., *The Romance of the Red Triangle* (London, Hodder & Stoughton, 1919)

Articles/Essays in Periodicals/Collections

Finlay, Frank, 'Casualty of War: The Hounding of German Scholars in the UK', *Times Higher Education Online*, 19 March 2015

Gregor, Neil, 'To the Victor the Spoils', *The Literary Review*, May 2014, pp.19–20

Harris, Carol, 'Foreign Fields: Physiotherapy's Links to the First World War', *CSP History*, Vol. 20, No. 8, 7 May 2014

'Health for War Service' Times (London, England), 2 September 1915:9, *The Times Digital Archive*, 19 March 2015

Liddle, Dr Peter, '1914–45: Severe Wounds for the Serviceman. Wartime Evidence', in Losowsky, Monty (ed.), *Getting Better: Stories for the History of Medicine* (Leeds, Medical Museum Publishing, 2007)

Morgan, Kenneth O., 'The Twentieth Century' in Morgan, Kenneth O. (ed.), *The Oxford History of Britain* (Oxford, OUP, 1984), pp.582–679

'Munitions Workers', *Yorkshire Post*, 7 August 1916, p.3

Rowley, Tom, 'The Grand Duchess and her Tommies', www.telegraph.co.uk/history/world-war-one/10900034/The-Grand-Duchess

Savage, Ruth, 'From the Cricket Field to the Battlefield' in RGS Alumni 1914 centenary magazine (see below in 'Special Issues' section)

Sheehan, John, 'How a Band of Grocers, Porters and Builders Became Heroes of War', *Harrogate Advertiser*, 16 April 2015, pp.16–17

Sheffield, Gary, 'The Centenary of the First Wold War: An Unpopular View', *The Historian*, Summer 2014, pp.22–26

Sheffield, Gary, 'The Myths of Gallipoli', *BBC History Magazine*, April 2015, pp.54–59

Waite, Colin, 'Harrogate Connection Prompts WW1 Search' in *Claro Ancestors*, Vol. 4, No. 1, February 2009, pp.9–11

'Winter in the Trenches', *The Times*, 23 March 2015, p.28

YMCA article on Betty Stevenson at
  https://archive.org/details/bettystevenson

Special Issues: Periodicals
Catholic Women's League, newsletter feature: 'History of CWL
  Services Committee', issue for 2014
*Ripon Grammar School: Commemorating the Centenary of World
  War One*: special issue of the magazine, 2014
Shot at Dawn: World War 100, *Daily Mirror*, 2 June 2014

Archives
Anon, diary in ms of a soldier in the Royal Horse Artillery
Anon: *Ghadar Heroes* (Bombay, People's Publishing House, 1945)
Campbell, Colina, diary in online 'Inside the First World War'
  project, 2015
Hansard report, 20 November 1918, Vol. 32, pp.332–6
Maps: Ripon camps and 1911 Ordnance Survey map at North
  Yorkshire Record Office
Ministry of Information, *His Majesty's Minesweepers* (London,
  HMSO, 1943)
Ministry of Works, *Richmond Castle* (London, HMSO, 1960)
Titley, Chris, *1914 in Yorkshire* (York, York Museums Trust, 2014)
University of Hull Library, *Percy Smith – prison photographs*
University of Leeds, Liddle Collection – material from the autograph
  book and transcribed interview with Ernest England

Websites
www.archaeologydataservices.ac.uk/archivedownload
https://archive.org/details/bettystevenson
www.archive.thetablet.co.uk
www.catholicwomensleague.org
www.harrogatepeoleandplaces.info/ww1
www.pastscapes.org.uk
www.telegraphmediagroup.com
www.theduchyvixen.com
www.warmuseum.ca/cwm/exhibitions/George Metcalf Archival
  Collection

Index